ADVANCE PRAISE FOR *TRIPOWER*

"As a collegiate hockey player and rower, I didn't think of core training when I moved into [performing] triathlons. Only when I suffered through several injuries that laid me up for almost two years, did I realize that core strength would not only make me faster, but also improve my body's ability to prevent and heal injury. I got started late on the *Tri Power* program last year, but it still enabled me to make Honorable Mention All American in 2006 and, given training splits on the bike, track, and pool, I'm confident I'll be making All American this year—and race more with far fewer injuries."

— **Charles Macintosh**
  Honorable Mention All American USA Triathlete (2006)
  Member of Team Enhance Triathlon Team NYC
  Member of Elysium Fitness Cycling Team

"As I get older, the line between training and injury becomes more difficult to straddle. I have discovered that strength training is the key to keep me strong and injury-free during the long triathlon season. Not only are there physical benefits, the psychological lift it gives me when I need to push through fatigue and out of my comfort zone is immeasurable."

— **Renee Meier**
  NYC Triathlon, 1st place Age Group (2005)
  NYC Triathlon, 2nd place Age Group (2006)
  Montauk Mightyman 1/2 Ironman, 1st place (2004, 2006)
  Mighty Hamptons, 1st place (2004, 2006)
  Vytra Tobay Triathlon, 1st place (2004)
  Mighty North Fork, 1st place (2003)
  Vytra Tobay, 1st place (2003)

ADVANCE PRAISE FOR *TRIPOWER*

"After a week packed with running and cycling, most of my Monday mornings are intimately spent unknotting my legs on the foam roller. Like a best friend with a sadistic edge, it hurts as good as a hard sprint session. But it's the best self-care for my ITB, glutes, and hamstrings (that get as tight as a taught derailleur cable). Tri Power details a terrific and easy-to-follow myofacial release program that leaves me feeling loose and flexible and ready for the next go 'round."

—**Stefani Jackenthal,** *elite endurance athlete and adventure journalist*
  Big Sur Trail Marathon, 1st place (2006)
  South African Augrabies Extreme Marathon, 1st place (2006)
  Costa Rica's The Costal Challenge, 2nd place (2006)
  All American USA Triathlete (2001)
  New York City Triathlon, 1st place (2001, 2002)

"I have followed a strength training program in the off-season for the past three years. Triathlons, particularly cycling in my case, tend to create muscle imbalances that I believe lead to an increased risk of injury. I want to compete in this sport for a long time, and a structured strength training program allows me to achieve a sense of muscular balance and improve my performance by addressing weaknesses first. Tri Power not only provides me with the opportunity to assess and evaluate my strength program, but it also provides a structured program that compliments traditional strength programming with non-traditional training protocols such as balance training, movement prep, and corrective flexibility training."

— **Robert Auston,** *amateur triathlete and cyclist*

ADVANCE PRAISE FOR *TRIPOWER*

"Tri Power protocols address the necessary components of injury prevention. Lack of neuromuscular coordination in traditional core training, namely effective core training, should be done in a challenging environment that incorporates balance and stability. Inefficient motor patterns can develop in static movement patterns, such as crunches.

Periodization through phased training as used in Tri Power is important for [your] body, particularly the nervous and muscular systems…. Traditionally endurance-related sports such as running, cycling, and triathlons have not [before] incorporated consistent power training in program design, for either misplaced safety or lack of knowledge… [It] increases your running form through greater nervous system recruitment."

— **Dr. Scott G. Duke DC, DACBSP,**

A graduate of the New York Chiropractic College
American Chiropractic Board of Sports Physicians Diplomat
Expert in the field of athletic and spine rehabilitation specializing in soft tissue management

"Having worked with hundreds of Olympic, national, and world class athletes, it is amazing to appreciate how finely attuned they are to small changes in their body. If we multiply the number of repetitions, as in the sport of Triathlon, times the abnormal forces acting on the body it is easy to understand how this could set up a soft tissue disaster. Tri Power addresses muscular imbalances, along with addressing the soft tissue changes, through a dynamic strength program designed for the everyday athlete.

Athletes who perform repetitive activities, such as triathletes, subject their musculoskeletal and myofascial systems to higher risk for injury. This repetition of movement creates continual biomechanical stress which for many athletes leads to breakdown of these soft tissue structures producing scar tissue."

— **Dr. Marc Jaffe**

United States team chiropractor for the 2003 World University Games in South Korea
United States Olympic Team Chiropractor for the 2004 Olympic Games in Athens, Greece
Diplomate of the American Chiropractic Board of Sports Physicians
2006 New Jersey Sports Chiropractor of the Year

TRIPOWER

TRIPOWER

The Ultimate Strength Training, Core Conditioning, Endurance, and Flexibility Program for Triathlon Success

Paul Frediani and William Smith

healthyliving**books**

New York • London

HatherleighPress
5-22 46th Avenue, Suite 200
Long Island City, NY 11101
www.hatherleighpress.com

Frediani, Paul, 1952-

 Tri power : the ultimate strength training, core conditioning, endurance, and flexibility program for triathlon success / Paul Frediani and William Smith.

   p. cm.

 ISBN 978-1-57826-244-1

 I. Triathlon--Training. I. Smith, William, 1976- II. Title.

 GV1060.73.F73 2007

 796.42'57—dc22

2007010536

DISCLAIMER

Before beginning any exercise program, consult your physician. The author and the publisher disclaim any liability, personal or professional, resulting from the application or misapplication of any of the information in this publication.

Tri Power is available for bulk purchase, special promotions, and premiums. For information on reselling and special purchase opportunities, call 1-800-528-2550 and ask for the Special Sales Manager.

Interior design by Allison Furrer, Jasmine Cardoza, and Deborah Miller
Cover design by Allison Furrer and Deborah Miller

10 9 8 7 6 5 4 3 2 1

Special thanks to New Balance for providing clothes and shoes for our *TriPower* photo shoot.

Printed in the United States

Table of Contents

Acknowledgments

The process of learning and sharing knowledge for enhancing the performance of the endurance athlete is an ongoing process. Everyone from researchers to athletes have their own opinions. We believe the information that we share with you in the following pages is both simple and applicable. We would like to acknowledge and thank the wonderful community of triathletes, medical professionals, and contributors that have spent countless hours reviewing *Tri Power's* protocols, and giving us advice on how to improve our program. Writing a book is a team effort which requires the help and support from many individuals. We'd like to thank:

Our editors, Alyssa Smith and Andrea Au

Our publishers, Andrew Flach and Kevin Moran, for seeing the value and benefit of publishing *Tri Power*

A great big thank you to our super models and triathletes, Sara Michaels and Steve 'Hulk' Muzzonigro, for demonstrating so eloquently *Tri Power's* exercises

Peter Peck, our photographer, for a 'great eye'

On a personal note, a special thank you to our families and friends that gave us their candid opinions for the last year and half on how to make *Tri Power* accessible and realistic for anyone, whether it's their first triathlon or their 10th.

Introduction

Triathlons are one of the most popular and accessible of sports. Regardless of age, sex, or athletic prowess, you can begin a training program that will lead you to the end of a successful race. Training for and competing in a triathlon gives you the satisfaction of completing a race and lets you walk away from it with a greater understanding of how your body functions and adapts to stress.

The vast majority of triathletes who compete recreationally are age groupers, or individuals with day jobs and families. Their most common complaint is that they do not have enough time to add strength training to their training program. After all, they are preparing for three different sports, and they feel their workout would be best spent swimming, biking, or running.

It's time to re-evaluate that train of thought. *Tri Power's* program is a valuable investment in your most important asset: your health. It will teach you discipline, self-respect, and commitment to your goals, all qualities that will take you far in any path of your life.

WHERE DID TRI POWER BEGIN (OR: WHY STRENGTH TRAINING)

We began to work together training adults for their first triathlons in May 2006. We weren't trying to make our clients into the next Olympic champions. Instead, we taught the health benefits of being a triathlete, how to train smart, and the best way to stay injury-free. We designed a road map to help each client find their inner voice that says, "I can, I will." Bobby McGee, a renowned coach and sports psychologist, once said, "Show them that training is only the process of learning to unlock that greatness that is within us all." We are delighted to share with you now the program we designed for our clients.

Our goal was for our clients to participate in the 1st Annual JCC Triathlon at the end of three months of training. With this in mind, we created a program that encompassed a weekly team training session supported by a motivated coach. We used extensive postural, flexibility, and strength assessments to determine current abilities.

Fifteen New York professionals were not going to take our advice as coaches at face value. They asked questions—lots of them. They prodded and challenged us every step of the way. No one in the class had ever done a triathlon before so the thought of doing a 1/2 mile swim, one-hour bike ride, and 3-mile run was daunting. As the training evolved, they saw results—and then what once seemed impossible seemed doable.

On August 7th at 7:10 A.M. sharp, 15 individuals jumped into the water for a 1/2 mile swim, and by 9 A.M., not only did we have doctors, teachers, psychologists, and stockbrokers in our midst, we had 15 triathletes.

WHO ARE TRIATHLETES?

Most triathletes are just like you—people with jobs and families who want to make health and fitness an integral part of their life. They want to be around other like-minded individuals in a supportive atmosphere. It really doesn't matter if you participate in a mini-distance sprint-triathlon or a full-blown Ironman, because in both, it's the first step that counts.

Triathletes know the challenge in front of them and accept it. They commit to a solid training schedule and see it through, demonstrating their dedication and persistence. Take your pick: swim, bike, or run. Chances are at least one of these events will pose a challenge to you and require additional work. Even the greatest obstacles can be conquered. Just ask one of our triathletes, Nancy Newhouse.

Nancy, age 57, had an uphill battle to her first triathlon. Three years before she attempted our program, she had severe back surgery that left her with no abdominal strength, extra weight, and a long and arduous rehabilitation. Nancy quickly became the inspiration of the group as she gained strength and mileage step-by-step. Did she have any doubts? You bet. A week before the triathlon she had problems sleeping. But she trusted in her training and completed her race. Now, she calls herself a triathlete.

The success of these 15 professionals helped prove that anyone can become a triathlete. Know that when you choose to complete a triathlon, you are committing to a healthier way of life. Remember to train smart, be consistent, listen to your body, and let *Tri Power* be your guide.

In Health and Fitness,

Paul & Will

The Program

1

HOW TO USE THIS BOOK: A GUIDE TO MAXIMIZING

Tri Power will provide you with the knowledge, guidance, and structure you need—while still allowing you to have a life! This is NOT a how to swim, bike, and run book. Training for a triathlon, especially your first, can be an overwhelming and involved process. This is a to-the-point and time-conscious program designed to keep you on the road—or in the water, if you're swimming laps.

 Tri Power follows a simple format that incorporates five elements: Beyond Stretching, Warm-Ups, Strength Development, Corrective Exercises, and Core Development.

Beyond Stretching

Have you ever said to yourself, "I stretch all the time! Why am I not getting any more flexible?" There is a way to increase your flexibility through improved knowledge of how your body functions. We will be introducing you to a foam roller (a long cylindrical object made of dense foam). This, and knowledge of your myofasical system (a network of tissue that wraps around your muscles, organs, bones, and the rest), will help you understand the relationship between parts of your body.

Warm-Ups

A lot of us grew up knowing we should stretch before participating in any activity. The end result of this is that we spend a lot of time preparing ourselves with stretches that have nothing to do with the movement patterns and intensity of exercise that is about to happen. In Warm-Ups, we will talk about balance between your muscle groups, the benefits of raising your body temperature to a vigorous sweat, and how to contract your muscles over multiple joints at once. We also call this movement preparation.

Strength Development

I'm sure you are saying to yourself, "I know what strength development is; I've been doing it all my life!" While we believe that to be true, *Tri Power* will be taking you through multiple patterns of movement with increased resistance. Triathlons generally require a forward motion, or an activity with very little lateral motion. Did you know that moving continuously in one pattern of movement creates imbalances in your body that can result in weak performance or injuries? In a triathlon, we react dynamically: running out of the water, sprinting out of the transition area, or slipping on a rock and catching our balance. Whatever the scenario, *Tri Power* will stimulate your body on this journey of movement through four phases of training: Foundations, Building, Power, and Maintenance.

Corrective Exercises

We all have different muscle weaknesses and restrictors. For example, weakness can appear in the form of recurrent lower back pain, and restrictors could be tight hamstrings pulling on your hips. In *Tri Power*, you will be shown strengthening and flexibility exercises that can be used based upon your individual needs in your strength program.

Core Development

Your core is not limited to your abdomen, but includes the entire area between your knees and shoulders, otherwise known as the connection between your lower and upper body. Your core strength is not only your abs, but also your groin, spine, and ribcage strength. *Tri Power's* goal is to build muscle from the inside (around your organs and spine) outward toward your abs. As you read further, you'll realize there is a strong connection between foam rolling exercises and the core.

Each of these five elements is included in the four strength phases. It's that simple: five components, four phases. These four phases of training will peak your conditioning for a single triathlon or for the full triathlon season. The phases (Foundation, Building, Power, and Maintenance) build your conditioning to give you the greatest chance for success with the least possible risk for injury. This progressive conditioning is known as periodization, or a way to rotate the phases of your training throughout your yearly training cycle. Like when you build a house, you begin with the foundation, then install the frame, insulations, and floors. It's only at the end that you paint and add the bells and whistles. If you skip a phase, your house may not stand the first time there is a storm.

A triathlete must condition for three sports, which is in itself time-consuming. However, our program will cut it down to basics and will take approximately three 30-minute workouts per week—all from home with minimal equipment.

Spending hours in a gym each week can feel redundant and ultimately ineffective. You probably think you're wasting a lot of

Breathing

As a rule, you should exhale during the exertion phase of an exercise. For example, in a squat, you should inhale before you begin the squat, brace your abs, and lower the weight. When you reach the bottom of your range of motion, you will return to the standing position while exhaling slowly. During a push-up, you will inhale when you lower yourself to the floor, then exhale as you push off the floor. Never hold your breath!

The Brace

If you've ever taken a class, you'll have heard the instructor say, "Tighten your abs!" Well, what exactly does that mean? Bracing your abs can protect your back from injury during strength training. You should be tightening your belly from the inside out. To do this, take a natural breath, allowing your abs to expand fully. Then, draw your belly button to your spine. Hold it there while continuing to breathe. This is a brace. What you've done is create intra-abdominal pressure, which is a stabilizing mechanism for the lower back.

strength program for the first time. Warm-Up, Strength, Core, and Beyond Stretching exercises are included.

Phase II: Building

During this phase, you will begin exercising through different patterns of movement, grow stability in your spine and hips, and increase the weight for all of these exercises. Holding the muscles under tension for longer periods of time will build strength and prepare you for the stretch-shortening cycle (SSC) in the next phase. As your muscles become stronger, they recover quicker from stress.

Phase III: Power

Power is the ability to move as quickly as possible within a given time period over a standard distance. This will be accomplished by strengthening the SSC, which is responsible for shortening and length mechanic in the muscle. In this phase, you'll discover why deceleration and recovery are so important for triathletes. This is also a factor in injury prevention and performance. After all, how much more fatigued does your body get running on sand than it does on concrete?

Phase IV: Maintenance

You've made it! Great job arriving to the Maintenance phase. At this point you will be entering your tri season and starting to see the benefits of your *Tri Power* program in

time—and you are. A well-designed strength and flexibility program should not take more than 30 minutes of real effort a few times a week. If you consider the long-term benefits, this small investment of time is well worth it.

THE FOUR PHASES OF TRI POWER

Phase I: Foundation and Adaptation

Before you begin working on strength and power, you need to make sure your foundation is secure. Think of your body like a tree. You have the stump, trunk, roots, and branches. We need to grow your foundation, and evolve the surrounding structures. In the Foundation phase, we introduce our action. During this phase, recovery and consistency are our priorities. The volume of exercises decrease, but you are swimming, biking, and running in full swing.

As you page through *Tri Power*, soak up all the knowledge and information at your own pace. Each circuit is progressive, challenging, and specific to your needs as a three-sport athlete. Yes, you are an athlete!

EQUIPMENT

Prior to using the *Tri Power* program it will be important to familiarize yourself thoroughly with the equipment contained in the following pages. *Tri Power* has gone through great efforts to not only explain exercises, but to show them via pictures in a manner conducive to even the most inexperienced fitness participant. With this in mind, explanations and pictures do not fully capture how to use a piece of equipment safely, so this is our goal in the paragraphs below. Please read our descriptions and suggestions for the physio-ball and elastic band several times.

The Physio-Ball

Because of the physio-ball's unstable nature, training on it strengthens your stabilizing muscles, the muscles that are found at major joints and around your spine, hips, and shoulders. It also conditions your body globally, as opposed to isolating muscle groups. This unique form of training will enhance your strength,

Height	Ball Size
Up to 4'10" (145 cm)	Small, 18" (45 cm)
4'10" – 5'5" (145–165 cm)	Medium, 22" (55 cm)
5'5" – 6'0" (165–185 cm)	Large, 26" (65 cm)
6'0" – 6'5" (185–195 cm)	X-Large, 30" (75 cm)

Sizing a Physio-Ball

Depending on your individual needs (sitting or exercising), you may need different sizes.

endurance, and balance by utilizing your neuromuscular system and how your nerves and muscles communicate.

We recommend you get acquainted with the ball first by performing exercises

Hip Hinging

You should remember to keep your torso tall and your spine straight to focus on bending or "hinging" forward at the hip in all forward-bending exercises. Bending properly at the hips makes it easier to keep your spine straight. When you hinge forward, be sure you maintain a slight bend in your knees. You should be careful to not bend too much, because the greater the bend in the knees, the less you will stretch your hamstrings, making the exercise less effective.

CORRECT

INCORRECT

CORRECT

INCORRECT

such as rhythmically bouncing up and down in a sitting position, which is a low-intensity movement. We also recommend using a quality physio-ball. It should be burst-resistant up to 500 lbs. Be sure the ball is inflated so that it is taunt. Wipe the ball clean after each workout.

Elastic Bands

Elastic resistance has been used in physical rehab for decades. There are many exercises that you can do with bands that cannot be reproduced with any other method. The band is able to reproduce the body's movements within their full range of natural motion—as opposed to a machine, which only allows movement in a fixed plane. Exercising with the band is time-efficient and portable. It requires more coordination and stabilization than your standard machine-based exercise. Free weights rely on gravity for resistance while an elastic band uses its resistive design.

Be sure to anchor the band securely before executing an exercise. Anchoring can be done by wrapping the band around a pole, through a door frame if on the road, or around the leg of your bed, which essentially creates a stable point that is fixed. Also be aware that although the bands are extremely durable, occasionally they will break. Examine the band right before each use. The manufacturer recommends wearing safety glasses.

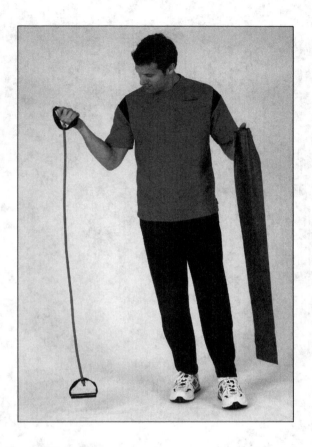

CONCLUSION

The most important tool you have is your body. Spend your time in this program with the understanding that each of us is unique, and thus your journey will be unlike anyone else's. What is the same is your commitment to evolve, change, and improve. So, when you're ready, jump on in—the water is great. Come and join the family of individuals that call themselves triathletes.

Strength and Flexibility Assessment
2

Strength training for triathletes is still in its infancy. If you mention strength training to an endurance athlete as a form of training, it brings to mind someone with huge muscles, who might lack flexibility, mobility, and endurance. While this is a form of strength training (known as bodybuilding), it's not the result you should seek as a triathlete.

Strength training for the triathlete should help to improve your performance skills and athletic movements. It's not gaining muscles for the sake of gaining muscles. This is the same misconception that kept baseball, basketball, tennis, and even football players out of the gym until the past few decades. Today, we know there is no sport that will not benefit from some kind of strength training.

Strength training for you, a triathlete, will help address muscular imbalances that lead to injuries, increase the ability to resist muscular fatigue, increase bone density, and enhance joint stability by strengthening muscles, ligaments, and tendons. A strength

training program will also improve power—that is, your ability to generate force. In triathlons, you'll be overcoming the water in the swim, the pedal during cycling, and the ground while running. We call this overcoming inertia. Strength training will also improve your movement efficiency; that is, the more efficient your movement, the less energy you expend, and the faster you will go.

Strength training will not cause weight gain, which can be a major issue for endurance athletes. In fact, after you hit age 30, your lean body mass (muscles) will decrease year by year, slowing down your metabolism and causing you to gain weight. Maintaining lean body mass through strength training will help you keep your weight down and strength up. If you don't strength train, you are more likely to gain the kind of weight you do not want: fat.

Strength training will not decrease your flexibility. Your muscles are tight for a reason, usually to guard another weak muscle group. For example, if your hip flexors are tight from extensive cycling, they will likely become tighter as the lower back becomes weaker. It's also important to mention that overly flexible muscles usually lead to instability in joints—something you don't want.

Tri Power's program is based around the specific physiological requirements of the sport and will result in the development of both power and muscular endurance. It's been designed to use training methods specific to triathlons, with the goal of reaching peak performance at the time of major competitions. In other words, *Tri Power's* specific strength programs will progress as you, the triathlete, progress. The workouts are designed to increase your performance through increased load, direction of movement, and types of resistance. You will never be bored. Don't dip the toe, jump right in the water with our first section: Assessment.

STRENGTH ASSESSMENT: BASELINE TO SUCCESS

Before beginning your program, you should assess exactly what you are bringing to the table. In addition to showing you where you need to go, at the end, it will show you just how far you've come. Everyone has injuries, genetic and congenital concerns, and varying levels of initial strength.

Follow this assessment along with the technique cues to give you a starting point before beginning the Strength phase of our program. There are pictures throughout to demonstrate correct form for each movement. This section will take you about 30 minutes. Good luck!

STRENGTH ENDURANCE ASSESSMENT

The following assessments should be done before embarking on a strength program. Only by assessing can you chart progress. The assessments should be done every four weeks.

The **TRIPOWER** Scorecard

Our scorecard is an excellent way to establish a baseline, re-evaluate, and determine progress throughout the year. The scorecard is also an important tool that can help the triathlete assess potential overtraining shortcomings by decreased strength numbers. Please feel free to copy this page and write directly on the sheet the results from our exercises.

Testing Exercises	Date	Date	Date	Date	Date	Date
Push-Ups: 60 Second Max Reps						
Wall Sit: Time to Exhaustion						
Flex-Arm Hang: Time to Exhaustion						
Side Plank: Time to Exhaustion						
Side Plank Bent Knee: Time to Exhaustion						
Prone Plank: Time to Exhaustion						
Extensor Chain: Neutral Plane is Broken						
Core Strength						

Strength Assessment
PUSH-UP

Lay on the floor and place your hands shoulder distance apart with your toes flexed. Push away from the floor and extend your arms fully. You should have a rolled towel under your chest. Lower yourself so that your chest touches the towel; your elbows should be bent to 90 degrees. Be sure to keep your head aligned with your spine and not sag at the hips. If you cannot keep this form perfect, then perform on your knees. We suggest using a mirror or partner for a form check.

RECORD: Number of Push-Ups in 60 seconds

TRI-DOG SAYS:
Feel this in your chest, shoulders, and stomach.

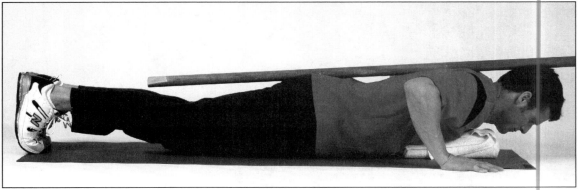

Strength Assessment
WALL SIT

Place a physio-ball between your lower back and a wall. Lower to a sitting position. The bottom of your thighs should be parallel to the floor and your knees should be directly over your ankles. Keep the chest high and your hands away from your thighs. Breath—do not hold your breathe.

RECORD: Time to exhaustion

TRI-DOG SAYS:
Feel this movement in your hips and thighs.

Strength Assessment
FLEX ARM HANG

Use a pull-up bar or a Smith machine. Use a chair to position yourself so that your chin is above the bar. Your palms should be facing you, and elbows fully flexed. The trick to executing this exercise correctly is 'locking in' your shoulder blades and keeping the elbows tight to the rib cage. Avoid kicking or swinging. Hold as long as you can.

RECORD: Time to exhaustion

TRI-DOG SAYS:
Feel this exercise in your arms and mid- and lower back muscles.

Strength Assessment
SIDE PLANK

Lay on side with legs stacked. Place your elbows directly under your shoulder. Lift hips off floor. Shoulders, hips, and legs must be in a straight line. Don't let your hips sag. Hold to exhaustion. Time both left and right sides.

RECORD: Time to exhaustion in correct form

TRI-DOG SAYS:
Feel this exercise in the side of your stomach (oblique) closest to the ground, and also the lower spine on the same side. Occasionally the triathlete will feel this exercise in the shoulder joint—don't worry; as long as your elbow is placed directly under your joint, it is safe. This will pass as your stomach and ribcage muscles get stronger.

Strength Assessment

SIDE PLANK BENT KNEE

Lay on side with legs stacked. Place your elbow directly under shoulder. Bend the bottom leg at the knee, keeping thighs parallel. Elevate hip off floor and extend and hold the top leg parallel to floor. Time both left and right sides twice.

RECORD: Time to exhaustion in correct form

TRI-DOG SAYS:
Feel this exercise in the hip closest to the ground, aka the bent knee hip. As with the previous Side plank, push your hips forward into a neutral spine. Feel this exercise on both sides of your hips around your glutes.

Strength Assessment
PRONE PLANK

Lay on stomach, place elbows directly under shoulders. Lift hips off floor. Press palms of hands together and imagine pulling elbows apart. Keep head, shoulders, and hips in a direct line. Do not allow the lower back to sag. Breathe. As you exhale, envision your navel pulling up and into your spine. Lower slowly to the ground if you feel back pain.

RECORD: Time to exhaustion in correct form

TRI-DOG SAYS:
Feel this exercise in the front stomach and leg muscles. Use a mirror to maintain a neutral spine. If you cannot maintain a neutral spine, the modification for this exercise is on your knees.

Strength Assessment

EXTENSOR CHAIN

Place hips on physio-ball or bench. Anchor heels on a bench or rail at or close to hip level. Hold torso parallel to floor. Hands are by thighs with palms rotated to floor and shoulder blades are squeezed together. Keep torso parallel to floor. Hold until your torso breaks horizontal plane.

RECORD: Time to exhaustion in neutral spine

TRI-DOG SAYS:
Having the ability to keep your body in a neutral position under load (aka against an external force like gravity) is key for spinal health and performance. Feel this exercise in the hamstrings, glutes, and torso muscles. If there is any pain behind the knees, visualize you're making yourself longer and flatter.

Strength Assessment
CORE STRENGTH

Lie on floor and place one hand, palm down, under back, directly behind navel. Bring legs to 90 percent perpendicular to floor. Maintain lower back pressure on hand. Slowly lower legs. Stop the moment you feel the lower back releasing pressure on the hand. Note the percentage you've lowered your legs.

RECORD: Percent of lower ab strength

 TRI-DOG SAYS:
Quite often we think we're strengthening the abs when in fact we're strengthening the hip flexor muscles. As the hip flexors are already strong from cycling they override the abdominals exacerbating lower cross posture.

Degrees Percent of Lower Ab Strength

Degrees	Percent of Lower Ab Strength
75°	50%
60°	60%
45°	70%
30°	80%
15°	90%
0°	100% (touching to the ground)

FLEXIBILITY ASSESSMENT

Flexibility is described as a muscle's ability to move over the surfaces it is attached to, ideally moving freely without restriction or pain. Restriction can occur because of chronic static positions, such as sitting for long periods of time, or general lack of movement. Pain can occur through trauma, accidents, or overtraining. Here, you will be taught how to assess your own flexibility, determine your restrictions, and apply the stretches most needed to enhance athletic performance and general function.

You'll begin to understand the application of flexibility and why it is important. Most important of all, you'll begin to understand how your body works together and how opposite muscle groups should be balanced. An example would be the hip flexors, which flex the hip, and the glutes, which pull your hip backward. We use these two muscle groups because they can have a direct effect on your triathlon experience if tight or weak.

Let's pose a scenario. You are on your bike and the powerful hip flexor muscle is working like crazy to pull the pedal upward, indirectly pulling on your lower spine. The glutes are working to stabilize the hip and pull the pedals backward, opposing the action of the hip flexors. Since the hip flexor muscle group in most humans tends to be extremely powerful and overactive, generally more active than the glutes, it will tighten up to protect itself from being overstretched. This guarding will make the glutes progressively weaker. By stretching the prime mover, in this case your hip flexors, the glutes will become more active by nature.

Who would have thought stretching a tight muscle could ever increase function in another muscle? Crazy, but true. Let's move onto the flexibility portion of *Tri Power* and see how you can realign your body.

Remember:

- DO breathe during all movements. Generally we will breathe out going into a stretch and breathe in returning to our starting position.
- DO hold your stretches for at least 30 seconds.
- DO drink half of your body weight in ounces of water every day, as this will affect the stretching capability of tissues such as muscle and skin.

- DO 'anchor' the joint closest to the body being stretched. For example, when stretching the side of your neck, keep your shoulders down. Do not allow the body to shift into the stretch.
- DON'T get up quickly from a stretch on the floor. NOTE: Older adults have a decreased fluid volume in the body. This leads to blood pooling and a wave of dizziness upon standing up. Strengthening the heart will help this blood return at a faster rate, hence a decrease in dizziness.

Flexibility Assessment-Neck

FORWARD HEAD POSTURE

TRI-DOG SAYS:
Proper positioning of the head and neck atop the shoulders will allow proper breathing and rotation of the torso during swimming. In addition, proper torso rotation will decrease strain on the rotator cuff and shoulder joint. Tri-Dog wants you to know that low back and neck pain are intimately related, and can contribute to decreased performance if the spine is not kept strong and flexible.

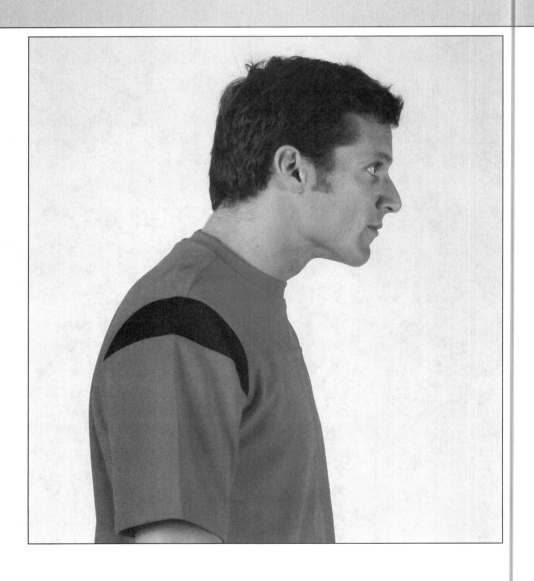

Flexibility Assessment-Neck
ASSISTED LATERAL FLEXION

In a sitting position (preferably), place the opposite hand of the side being stretched on the side of your head. Rest the nonworking hand at your side. This position relaxes the larger muscle groups around the neck. Proceed to drop your ear toward the base of the opposite shoulder. It's very important to keep a neutral neck position.

CORRECTIVE STRETCH

Flexibility Assessment-Neck

LATERAL FLEXION

TRI-DOG SAYS:
During all three sports, especially swimming and biking, the back of the neck becomes extremely tight. Stretching the back of the head and neck allows the shoulders and back to relax during all three sports, which will allow for better body mechanics.

Flexibility Assessment-Neck
ASSISTED NECK FLEXION

In a sitting position, relaxing the hips and legs, place one hand on your chest, opposing hand behind the head. Gently breathe out and drop your chin forward while simultaneously extending the back of your head out. Feel a stretch through upper back of the neck, even through the upper back between your shoulder blades. An important safety point to be aware of is not to pull or push the head into a stretched position. Rather, allow the breathing to gently coordinate the slow stretch of the neck. Imagine a giraffe's neck elongating.

CORRECTIVE STRETCH

Flexibility Assessment-Shoulders

ARM UNDER

TRI-DOG SAYS:
Maintaining range of motion in the shoulders helps to create longer and smoother swimming strokes. A smoother stroke makes a triathlete glide and rotate in the water by requiring less energy through improved technique.

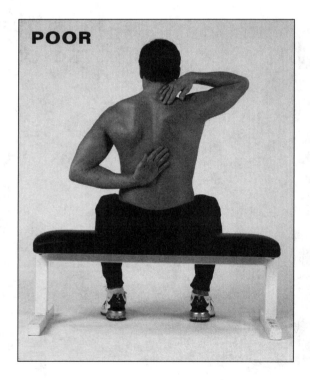

POOR

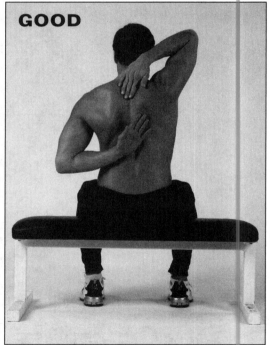

GOOD

Flexibility Assessment-Shoulders
ARM UNDER WITH TOWEL

Sitting down is a great position for this stretch, as it truly isolates the upper body. Keep the top elbow pointed up, not out, and the bottom elbow pointed out and tight to the body. Breathe in and gently contract your upper back and pull with the top hand. You will feel a stretch in the front of the bottom shoulder.

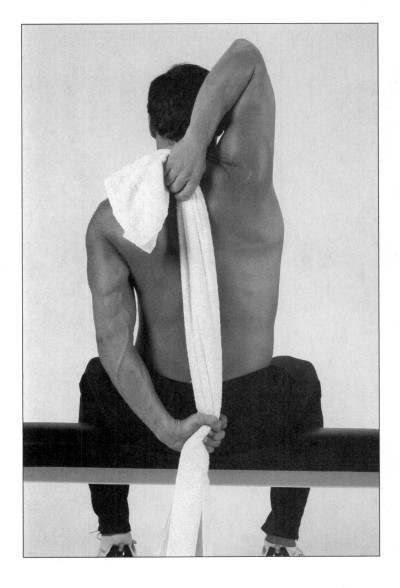

CORRECTIVE
STRETCH

Flexibility Assessment-Shoulders

ARM OVER

TRI-DOG SAYS:
Maintaining range of motion in the shoulders helps to create longer and smoother swimming strokes. A smoother stroke makes a triathlete efficient in the water by requiring less energy.

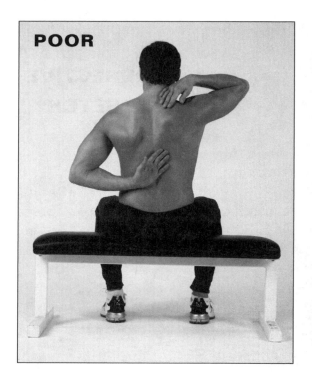

POOR

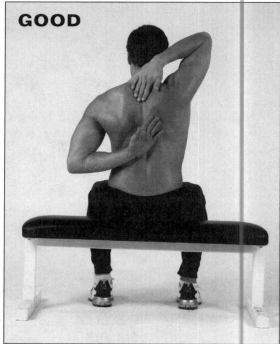

GOOD

Flexibility Assessment-Shoulders
ARM OVER WITH TOWEL

Sitting down is a great position for this stretch, as to truly isolate the upper body. Keep the top elbow pointed up, not out, and bottom elbow pointed out and tight to the body. Breathe in and gently contract your upper back and pull with the bottom hand. You will feel a stretch in the side/bottom of the top shoulder.

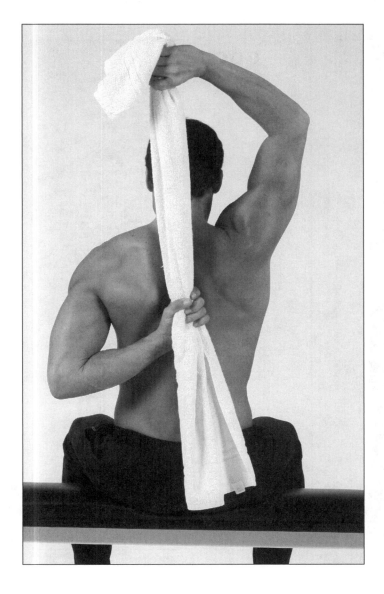

CORRECTIVE
STRETCH

Flexibility Assessment-Shoulders

OVERHEAD 180

TRI-DOG SAYS:
All three sports require a different shoulder response during training. In swimming, the overhead movement is the most important indicator of shoulder mechanics and strength in the surrounding shoulder muscles.

POOR

GOOD

Flexibility Assessment-Shoulders

TWO HAND OVERHEAD PUSH

This corrective stretch displays if the traithlete has possible neck pain by contracting both sides of the neck together. Gently push the palms together, breathe out, and push the hands upward. Feel stretch outside the lower shoulder blades.

TWO HAND OVERHEAD INTERLOCKED PALM PUSH

Begin by rotating your arms inward and interlocking the fingers. The interlocked palms are brought directly over the head. Push the palms upward, emphasizing the pull from the shoulder blades and ribcage. The triathlete can perform this stretch standing in a slight squat or sitting on a stable surface.

CORRECTIVE STRETCHES

Flexibility Assessment-Chest
LYING DOWN TWO-ELBOW DROP

TRI-DOG SAYS:
Triathletes with flexibility in the front of their pec/shoulders will have better posture and less rotator cuff and shoulder pain.

POOR

GOOD

Flexibility Assessment-Chest

ARM STRETCH

Position your body to the side of the ball. Place your arm across the top of the ball with your elbow resting on the apex. Keeping your arm straight, back rounded, abs in, and eyes on the ground in front of you, roll the ball further out toward your hand and feel the stretch in your shoulders.

PHYSIO-BALL PEC STRETCH

Your head and shoulders will be relaxed on the physio-ball, with the hips and lower back gently curving over the ball. Arms will be extended out to the side, feeling a stretch through the front of the shoulders and chest area.

CORRECTIVE STRETCHES

Flexibility Assessment-Lower Back
SIT AND REACH

TRI-DOG SAYS:
Triathletes will warm-up, train, and recover at a faster rate if their lower back is more flexible. Residual soreness and fatigue from a restricted lower back will contribute to resulting tightness in hip flexor and hamstring muscle groups.

Flexibility Assessment-Lower Back

CHILD'S POSE

Begin on all fours. Drop your hips back over the feet without moving the hands. Relax the upper body with smooth breathing as the body moves backward. A long stretch will be felt in the outer and lower back. Imagine walking your hands away from your lower back as the hips go toward the ground. A variation of this exercise for a triathlete with impingement or pain in the shoulder is to rotate the palms toward each other while dropping backward.

CAT STRETCH

Begin on all fours. Imagine someone walking their fingers up and down your spine. As the back arches, tuck the chin in toward the chest while breathing out. As the back arches down, extend the chin out, and proceed to breathe in.

CORRECTIVE STRETCHES

Flexibility Assessment-Lower Back
SPINAL TWIST

TRI-DOG SAYS:
Proper rotation of the hips and trunk on top of each other is vital in swimming, but also for overall back and hip flexibility.

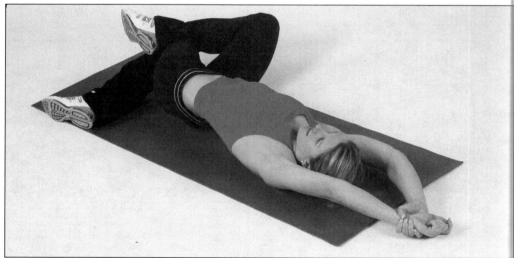

Flexibility Assessment-Lower Back
SEATED BENT KNEE

Bend the knee of the opposite side to be stretched. Cross the bent knee leg over a straight leg. Apply pressure to the outside of the bent knee, breathe out, and rotate across the body.

Flexibility Assessment-Hamstrings

SUPINE STRAIGHT LEG RAISE

TRI-DOG SAYS:
Tri-Dog believes a majority of lower back and hip problems start in the hamstrings, three muscles in the back of the leg. He also says runner's knee is partially caused by tight hamstrings.

Flexibility Assessment-Hamstrings
SUPINE BENT KNEE PULL

Lay on the ground. The non-stretching leg relaxes in a straight position with the toe pointing up. Pulling the stretching leg to the chest, bend the knee and keep the pelvis flat. Position a rope or towel in the midsole of the foot, gently pulling the foot over the hip, keeping the knee bent.

CORRECTIVE STRETCH

Flexibility Assessment-Gluteals

INTERNAL AND EXTERNAL HIP ROTATORS

TRI-DOG SAYS:
Triathletes have historically neglected the deep hip rotator muscles, namely the cuff the connects to the top of the femur or upper leg bone. They are important for stabilizing the body during all three sports, especially running, when the foot makes contact with the ground.

INTERNAL INCORRECT

INTERNAL CORRECT

EXTERNAL INCORRECT

EXTERNAL CORRECT

Flexibility Assessment-Gluteals

PRONE BENT KNEE SPLIT STRETCH

Begin on the floor, with legs in front. Drag one leg behind the body and gently bend both knees, being careful not to strain the knees in the setting-up stage. Keep the back upright and push the upper body out over the knee. Feel the stretch behind the hip of the front leg.

CORRECTIVE STRETCH

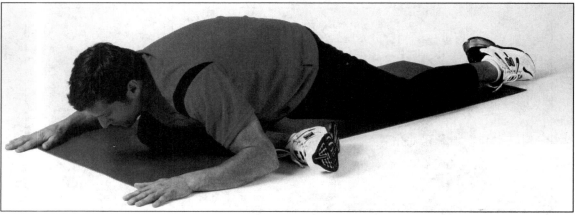

Flexibility Assessment-
Hip Flexors/Quads/IT Bands

THOMAS TEST

TRI-DOG SAYS:
Triathlon by nature is a sport of overusing certain patterns of movement, which makes stretching for all three sports very important. Lower Cross Syndrome, lower back concerns, and runner's knee can develop without proper stretching of the hips.

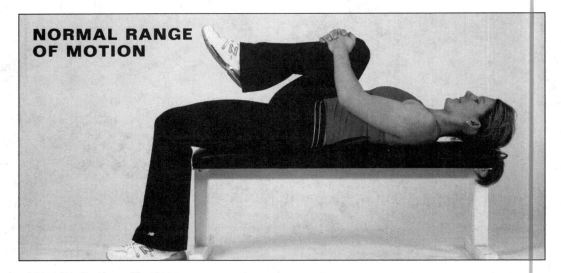

NORMAL RANGE OF MOTION

TIGHT HIP FLEXORS/QUADS

Flexibility Assessment-
Hip Flexors/Quads/IT Bands

SPLIT LEG HIP PUSH

Assume a lunge position. Shoulders should be positioned directly over the hips. Contract the back of the hip on the side being stretched, then push the hip forward, keeping a neutral lower-back position. Feel this stretch in the groin and quad of leg behind the body.

LATERAL KNEE PULL

Excellent stretch for the quads. Begin the stretch on the side of the body opposite the quad to be stretched. Reach back for the shoelaces and begin to pull back the knee by contracting the back of the hip or glute being stretched, as this will push the hip forward for a greater stretching sensation. Feel this in the front of the quad.

CORRECTIVE STRETCHES

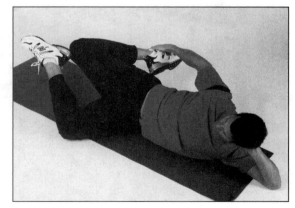

Flexibility Assessment-Calves

CALVES ASSESSMENT

TRI-DOG SAYS:
The calves are a sorely neglected area of the triathlete when it comes to power and stability. Our calves propel us forward and stabilize our entire leg and hip, particularly in the running and biking components of triathlon. Keep them flexible and strong! Under 6 inches means poor flexibility.

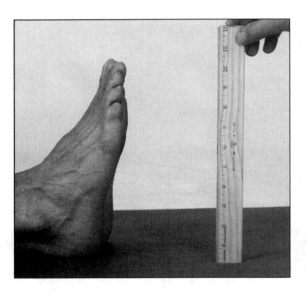
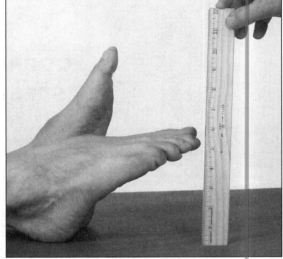

Flexibility Assessment-Calves
DOWNWARD DOG BIPEDAL HOLD

Have you ever seen the downward dog position in yoga? Well, during this particular stretch we will be stretching our calves out one at a time with a slight shifting of the hips down through the heel of the leg being stretched. To feel a more intense stretch, contract the front of the leg (quad) as you are pushing down with the heel.

**CORRECTIVE
STRETCH**

Components and Warming Up

3

When you warm up, you prepare your muscles for the activity you are about to perform. Your heart rate and awareness of your body begin to increase, and light perspiration should appear after just 5 minutes. It takes such a little amount of time, and it's so crucial for success. Some of the benefits include:

Exciting the Nervous System. Yes, your muscles are kind of stupid. They will basically do whatever you tell them to attempt. The more rapidly you can get your nerves to fire or turn on, the faster your muscles will respond—and with greater accuracy. During a triathlon you will constantly be asking your muscles to turn on and respond quickly. We teach the body how to do this through movement prep.

General Body Warm-up. A general warm-up cue is a light sweat. This means your core body temperature has risen around 2 degrees. With the core temp up, your blood flow has increased, joints are beginning to lubricate, and nutrients are delivered to working systems (lungs, kidneys, etc.) at a much faster rate then resting.

Balance and Coordination. Elizabeth Quinn, an exercise physiologist, has this to say about incorporating balance into your workouts: "Pain caused by sprained ankles and a variety of other injuries common to highly trained athletes often has nothing to do with strength. [Sprains and strains] often have little to do with flexibility. And rarely do they have anything to do with endurance. More often than not, sprains and strains have to do with balance." Balance training can help you prevent injury.

By performing a movement prep circuit several times per week for a maximum of 10 minutes, a triathlete will be thoroughly prepared mentally and physically for training, strength training, or supplemental exercise. Listen to Tri-Dog—he is smart—and remember, all of these exercises translate into a more natural and pain-free resting existence for you, the triathlete.

Warm-Up Exercises

ROTATOR CUFF

Stand with your elbows at a 90-degree angle and parallel to their corresponding shoulder. Begin to rotate the head of your arm bone by initiating movement with a closed fist. Perform this movement in an alternating fashion, then a coordinated fashion.

Warm-Up Exercises

BOOKENDS

Flexibility in the shoulders and chest is extremely important. Lay on your side with the hands on top of eachother. Gently open up the shoulders while keeping the opposite knee on the ground.

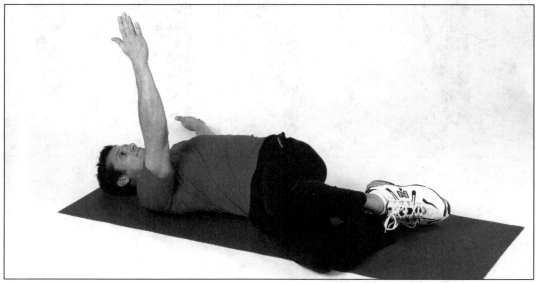

Warm-Up Exercises

SHOULDER GIRDLE

Ever seen March of the Wooden Soldiers? You are about to become a marching triathlete. Imagine a cross-country skier with the long arm motions during a smooth forward and backward arm swing. You will follow this smooth arc through the entire range of motion, allowing the hands to travel behind the hips then over the shoulder. Motion will be alternating to start, then moving into coordinated movement.

Warm-Up Exercises
CAT STRETCH

Position yourself on all fours with your hands under the shoulders and knees under the hips. Breathe out and arch the back like a scared cat. Upon reaching your absolute arch, breathe in and arch the spine the opposite direction, looking outward.

Warm-Up Exercises

HURDLER WALK

Position yourself with a wide hip stance. Keep your hands outside the hips so that the rotating hip has a cue on how far to rotate outward. Lift the knee upward and draw the knee across the body.

Warm-Up Exercises

CRADLERS

(A) Begin by crossing the ankle over the opposite knee. This is a Cradler. (B) Walking pulls can be executed by 'cupping' the knee and ankle in both hands while pulling the leg upward with the hip. (C) Dynamic skips involve no hands but rather an increased hip rotation with the feet spending very little time on the ground between reps.

Variations: Walking Pulls and Dynamic Skips

Warm-Up Exercises

ROTATIONAL TRUNK MOVEMENTS IN PLACE

Starting position for this stretch will be standing upright, moving arms through space in front of the body. Progressions will lead the triathlete into a leaning position, with the knees bent, rotating the body.

Warm-Up Exercises
SUPINE/PRONE LEG SWINGS

Perform this movement at a moderate pace that can be easily controlled. Face upward with the hands out to the side and palms down. Imagine your hips are the rotational point. Contract the stomach then swing the foot toward the opposite hand, and rotate sides. Repeat the same protocol but perform on your stomach.

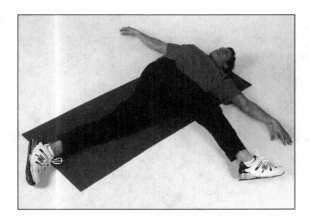

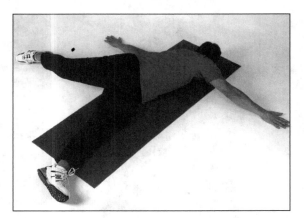

Warm-Up Exercises

STAR

Begin in a half-squatting position with the hands on the front of the thighs. Drop the hips down into a moderately deep squat then follow with the arms and hands touching the ground between the feet. Finish the motion by pushing the heels into the ground, breathe out, and open the arms up into a star position, ending in a standing position.

Warm-Up Exercises

ELBOW LUNGE

The triathlete will complete a normal lunging motion but with a bent elbow coming into the motion from the same side as the forward foot. Breathe out as you ease into the motion. A variation of this exercise for those not as limber has one hand resting on the ground.

VARIATION

Warm-Up Exercises

HANDS UNDER TOES/SUMO COMBO

Assume a standing position with the feet just inside the hips. Squat down and grab under the toes. Keeping the hands under the toes, straighten the knees. Feel a stretch through the hamstrings. Drop back into a squatting position, keeping your elbows between the knees.

Warm-Up Exercises

CARIOCA

Find a straight 15-yard runway. This dynamic movement will be a warm-up for the hip flexors and rotators. Bring the foot to the hand, not hand to the foot. Alternate feet to the opposite hand. Spend less time on the ground with the feet between touches, and increase the frequency of foot contacts as the movement continues.

Warm-Up Exercises

WALKING SINGLE LEG/ HAMSTRING STRETCH

The warm-up movement will be executed moving backward. Triathletes will feel a tremendous stretch behind the supporting leg. Extend the arms and leg together using the back and hip muscles.

Warm-Up Exercises

BALLISTIC HAMSTRING KICK

Remember neutral spinal position as you perform this exercise. Spinal position will be especially important during this movement. Find a wall and position your hands flat on the surface. Straighten the arms and keep them straight throughout the motion. Utilizing one leg at a time, slowly begin to snap the heel of the working leg up to the hip. As the hamstring loosens up, increase the speed until a ballistic heel kick is up to full velocity.

BEYOND STRETCHING: MYOFASCIAL RELEASE

Have you ever felt a knot between your shoulders that no amount of stretching or yoga would release? Do your lats feel as tight as piano strings after long swim sessions? Are your calves chronically sore? Has biking and running made your IT bands as tight as rubber bands? Then you will find relief with a self-massage technique (SMT). In recent years the sports medicine community has discovered the importance of the fascial system and its importance for optimizing performance and prevention of chronic injuries.

The body, from head to toe, is encased in a specialized tissue called fascia. Every muscle, nerve, organ, and blood vessel is encased in fascia. Gil Hedley, a nationally renowned researcher on the fascia, describes the human body as a twisty balloon, fascia being the balloon, and our muscles, bone, and organs being the air.

Everything in our body is one unit working together. Fascia can cause a sense of stuckness, tightness, adhesiveness—you name it. We cannot tell you how many times we've been told, "I never thought I could improve my flexibility. I stretch every day." More likely than not, your fascial system is stuck from lack of consistent and diverse movement and overuse from repetitive movement patterns.

Fascia has three layers. The first layer contains fat, nerve endings, blood vessels, and tiny muscles, and lies between the skin and the second layer. The second layer lies on top of the muscles and can be disrupted. The third and deepest layer wraps around the organs of your body.

Myofascial release concentrates on the first and second layers, although the effects will be felt throughout. While fascia is very pliable and relaxed, it can become constricted due to overuse or trauma. It can cause muscle pain, soreness, a reduced range of motion, and increased tightness. If these regions are not addressed, you could find yourself in an injury cycle caused by compensation and early muscular fatigue.

By using a foam roller on a regular basis and before or after your training sessions, you can alleviate or release these restrictions and muscle knots. By slowly kneading on a foam roller, you will release tightness, breaking down adhesions and restoring a full range of motion. An aligned body will improve performance. It will also decrease recovery time from workouts by improving circulation.

Triathletes will find sore spots in such areas as above the outside of the calf, between the knee and hip, and the front of the chest.

HOW YOU DO IT:

1. Maintain each position and roll along the roller for 1 to 2 minutes at a time.
2. When you reach a sore or painful spot, stop the roller and hold the position for 45 seconds or until the pain diminishes by 50 percent.
3. Be sure to keep your abs braced, maintaining good posture and even breathing.

HOT SPOTS:

Calves. Place back of calves on roller. Lift hips off floor and roll both sides of calves. Keep feet relaxed. For a more intense massage, cross one leg over the other and apply pressure with top leg.

Hamstrings. Place the back of your thighs on a roller. Roll from above the knees to your hips. Tightening the quadriceps while rolling on the hamstrings will increase massage.

Latisimus Dorsi. Place the side of your chest on the roller with your arm extended over your head. Keep thumb pointing up.

IT Band. Place the outside of your bottom thigh on the roller. Place elbow on floor for stabilization. Roll from hips to knee.

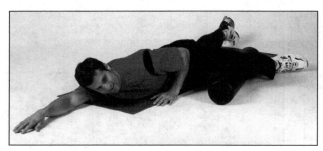

Adductors. Place your stomach comfortably on the ground. Relax your head on your hands, looking to the side. Place the inside of the groin, closer to the knee, on the foam roller. Ease into position as this spot will produce substantial discomfort during the onset.

Quadriceps. Place the front of your thighs on the roller. Roll from hips to knees.

Piriformis. Sit on roller with one foot crossed over the opposite knee. Roll on to the bent knee side.

Rhomboids. Place your shoulder blades on roller. Fold arms across chest and lift hips off floor for increased pressure.

YOUR CORE

The core is much more than just the abdominals. The simplest explanation of your core is the central, or most important, part. For example, the apple. You wouldn't look at the apple from the outside and call that its core. For an apple to be rich and delicious it must be healthy from the inside out. How often have you bought a beautiful shiny apple only to bite into it and discover it is rotten in the middle? Looks can be deceiving. You as a triathlete want your core not only to look strong but to be strong. Your core can only achieve the strength and endurance it needs by building its strength from the inside out.

Core Strength for the Triathlete

The core is the link that connects the movements of the upper and lower body. It flexes, extends, and rotates the torso for all three elements of a triathlon. Its primary function is having the endurance necessary to stabilize and protect your spine and lower back for extended periods of time. Core fatigue will destroy the efficiency of movement, create risk of injury, and result in poor performance.

The outer core is designed for powerful hip-to-shoulder rotational movement. Watch a sprinter or boxer and notice the abdominal muscles, defined and cut. They must be very strong for short and explosive movements. The abs of triathletes are toned, but do not have the definition of sprinter abs. This is because it is more important for the triathlete to have a strong inner core. The core of triathlete must be more fatigue-resistant than explosive. The longer the triathlon, the less important it is to perform explosive training for the core. It is the inner core that is the foundation for endurance sports. Like the cables of a bridge, it must be strong to maintain the integrity and stability of the trunk. The inner core must be strong first to stabilize the outer core. The inner and outer cores working together are the center of power and gravity and play an essential role in good balance and equilibrium.

The deepest of abdominal muscles is known as the transverses (TVA). It is a thin sheet of muscle to the sides of the rectus (six-pack) that joins the connective tissue behind it. The transverse is the only abdominal muscle with strictly horizontal muscle fibers. Acting as your body's natural corset, the TVA is the main muscle that pulls in your gut. Whenever your body moves, the TVA fires first—even before leg and arm movements—followed by the internal obliques, external obliques, and mult fidi muscles of the back. Only then does the most superficial muscle of the abs, your six-pack, fire.

If the transverses, internal obliques, or external obliques are weak, then all your movements will also be weak. It is your deep core musculature that will keep you from straining your back during your triathlon when you're maintaining a fixed posture for an extended period of time.

The transverses are assisted by the main trunk stabilizers, or the internal oblique muscles. The fibers of the internal obliques provide a layer of support over the horizontal transverses fibers. An important concept here to grasp is that the internal obliques on one side of the body work with the superficial external obliques on the opposite side. If you are dominant on one side of your body, as all of us generally are, early fatigue can happen during rotational movements such as swimming. You may also find it harder to breathe on one side of your body than another. We will address these deficiencies in our training program.

Most abdominal routines focus on developing a six-pack. It's the main abdominal muscle that you can see, which is why we all seek to develop that area. Unfortunately the result of doing countless reps of crunches is a minor increase in abdominal strength and a minimal decrease in the girth of the waistline. The six-pack has nothing to do with a flat stomach or tight gut. The primary function of the six-pack is to flex the trunk so that your rib cage moves toward the front of your legs. Not only that, but a strong core has nothing to do with low body fat levels. Abdominal definition is the result of diet, not torso work.

When the inner and outer cores effectively work together, they can stabilize the back and hips. This can also help with your breathing patterns. The co-contraction between the inner and outer cores creates one of the most powerful triathlon-specific movements: the shoulder-to-hip rotation you apply in sprint or in Olympic distances. You will use your core many times in a triathlon, from the shoulder and hip coordination during powerful rotations, getting away from a pack in the swim, cranking hard on the pedals up a hill, or sprinting to the finish line.

Core conditioning has to be placed at the top of every triathlete's priority list. Muscular imbalances, early fatigue, and poor posture can result from a lack of core strength. The *Tri Power* core training will address the inner core first, creating the core on the foundation of stability, strength, and endurance.

THE FINAL COMPONENT: BREATHING

There's one component people may just assume they have under control. After all, you've been breathing since your first day on this earth. What if we told you that most people have an inverted breathing pattern, and by reverting back to their natural pattern of breathing, they can enhance oxygen intake?

Here's a simple test. Place your hand on your stomach and take a big breath. What did your stomach do as you inhaled? Did it expand or did it suck in? If your stomach sucked in, you have inverted breathing, or an upper chest breathing pattern.

An upper chest breathing pattern causes a buildup of toxins in the body, primarily carbon dioxide. As carbon dioxide increases within our system, our breathing rate increases to handle the demand of expelling toxins. During a race, you want to breathe as fully and relaxed as possible. Taking quick shallow breaths increases the level of carbon dioxide in your blood, causing your arteries to constrict and reducing the flow of blood through the body. Ultimately, this will cause you tension and anxiety.

Your diaphragm is a muscle that sits flat across your body, separating the lungs from your organs. It's like the skin of a drum stretching under the ribcage. For your lungs to fully expand, your diaphragm must fall lower, thus pulling air into your lungs. As the diaphragm lowers, the abdominal region will swell.

There are three separate levels of breathing. They are known as belly (diaphragmatic), chest (intercostal), and shoulder (clavicular). The ideal breath combines all three. It begins at the belly when the breath is drawn in. The diaphragm lowers and the abdominal region swells. Good breath control starts here. Once the abdominal region swells, the chest expands, achieved by the rise of the chest and expansion of the ribs. It's quite common for athletes to be chest breathers; however, it takes more effort and allows less air to enter. Lastly, raising the shoulders and collarbone while inhaling is known as the clavicular breath (where only the upper lungs are fully functional). A complete breath begins at the diaphragm, swells the abdominals then the chest and ribs naturally, allowing the lungs to completely fill up to the collarbones.

Observe a baby or even your pet dog or cat when he or she is sleeping. He or she breathes in and the little belly expands. As he or she exhales the belly becomes smaller. This is a perfect breath, no physical or physiological stress. The stomach is relaxed, and the rib cage is flexible with no tension, just pure natural uninhibited breath.

Practice your own breathing by lying on your back. Place one hand over your navel. Inhale, allowing your breath to fill the belly, then the chest. During the inhale, you should relax the abs and obliques. Relax and do it again. Try to get your head out of the exercise; your thinking will just get in the way of what the body will naturally do. Always practice your breathing in private. The average resting rate of breath at rest is 10 times a minute.

TRIPOWER
Phase 1: Foundation and Adaptation

4

Whether you're an experienced triathlete or a beginner, Phase I is where your training begins. In this phase, you will create a foundation that will allow you the best chance of having an injury free and successful triathlon season. If you're an experienced triathlete, it is Phase I where you allow your body the time needed to recover and recuperate from the physical stress of the season.

In Phase I, you address your flexibility needs and begin the process of developing muscular, ligament, and tendon strength. Ligaments connect bone to bone and tendons connect muscles to bones. With proper training, ligaments and tendons, like muscles, will increase in strength. An imbalance of strength can cause injury. If you strain a muscle it will recover to pre-injury level, not so with ligaments and tendon. In Phase I we begin slowly strengthening the ligaments, tendons and deep postural and stabilizer muscles around joints.

Generally speaking, we have two types of muscle fibers. They are 'fast twitch' and 'slow twitch.' Fast twitch (or type 2) do not require oxygen, are fast to fatigue, and are more powerful than slow twitch muscle fibers. Slow twitch (type I) muscle fibers are slow to fatigue and rely on oxygen to produce energy. Regardless of any physical movement you make, the slow twitch fibers fire first, even if just briefly, to stabilize and prepare the limbs for movement.

Envision a chicken and a duck. You may remember in the movie *Rocky*, he was training to increase foot speed by attempting to catch a chicken. Chickens move quickly but fatigue fast, so they can only fly a few feet at a time. Think of chickens as your fast twitch muscle fibers. A duck, on the other hand, is relatively slow when walking but can fly for hundreds of miles without stopping. Think of a duck as your slow twitch muscle fibers.

In Phase I you will train predominately with only your body weight—which in the end is the only weight you will be carrying in the race. The tempo of the exercises is rather slow in this phase (3:I:3). This places your body under stress for a longer period of time, thus developing the deep stabilizing and postural muscular strength you need for further strength development.

Foundations Phase

Length: 2 Months

Foundations will be your first exposure to the Tri-Power method of progressive and structured strength development. This phase is about connecting with your body, finding the strengths and weaknesses that are inherent in each of us. Become used to completing a workout in its entirety and feel the sense of accomplishment that goes along with it. Between each set you are moving around, breathing well, and focusing on your next exercise.

You will see that in the all the phases (Foundation Phase) we have set an option of how many repetition/time and sets you have the option of completing per phase. This is specifically designed as not to be a 'cookie cutter' program. Essentially regardless of your current conditioning level you can adjust the intensity of the program by following the lower to higher volume (reps x sets) recommendation in each phase. We do ask you to strictly adhere to the Tempo or speed prescribed per exercise. A 3/1/2 Tempo means each repetition would be 6 seconds in length, or three seconds on the pulling part of the exercise (raising a dumbbell/bodyweight/bungee), one on the top of the movement (holding the dumbell/bodyweight/bungee), and two on the recovery part (lowering the dumbbell/bodyweight/bungee).

Complete the weekly schedule one week at a time, and evaluate your progress at the end of the week by using the Strength and Flexibility Assessments.

MONDAY/WEDNESDAY/FRIDAY	
Corrective Flexibility Movements:	**5 Minutes**
Perform 30 second holds of each exercise, then repeat. You should apply the corrective movements you most need based upon your self-administered assessments. We suggest performing the following sections together as their function relates:	

Symptom	Area
poor upper body score	Neck/Shoulders/Chest stretches
poor mid/lower back score	Lower Back/Hamstring/Calf stretches
poor hip/lower body score	Glutes/Hip Flexors/IT-Band/Quad stretches

Core:	**5 Minutes**
Perform 30 repetitions or seconds of the following exercises, then repeat without pausing.	

TVA Activation	The Brace	Hip Bridge	Superman	Lateral Ball Rolls

Myofascial:	**5 Minutes**
Perform 30 seconds of the following movements, then repeat. This should be the last piece of your workout.	

Calves	Hamstrings	Latisimus Dorsi	IT Band

TUESDAY/THURSDAY

Movement Preparation:	5 Minutes

Perform 10 reps of the following exercises, then repeat. For single leg movements, perform 5 reps of each leg.

Cat Stretch   Shoulder Girdle   Hurdler Walk   Cradlers

Foundations Strength Training Phase:	30 minutes

The length of the workout is contingent upon your current level of conditioning. Your level of strength conditioning was determined by the strength assessment completed at the beginning of this book. Increase the repetition and sets accordingly.

Exercise	Repetitions	Sets	Load	Rest	Tempo
PUSH (All)					
Push-Up	5-10	1-3	Bodyweight	1 minute	3/1/2
PULL (1 of 3)					
Flex Arm Hang	Hold to exhaustion		Bodyweight	1 minute	Hold to exhaustion
Lat Pulldown	10-15	1-3	65-75% Max	1 minute	3/1/2
Pull-Up	3-6	1-3	Bodyweight	1 minute	3/1/2
SQUAT (1 of 3)					
Front Squats	10-15	1-3	65-75% Max	1 minute	3/1/2
Static Lunges	10-15	1-3	Bodyweight to 65-75% Max	1 minute	3/1/2
*Prone Manual	15	1-3	Bodyweight	1 minute	3/1/2
LIFT (1 OF 2)					
**Deadlift	15	1-3	Bodyweight to 65-75% Max	1 minute	3/1/2
Single Leg Deadlift	15 per leg	1-3	Bodyweight to 65-75% Max	1 minute	3/1/2

*Prone Manual must be performed 1 out of 2 Strength Conditioning days.
**Make sure to have perfected your form before adding weight to your load.

SATURDAY

Sport Specific Skill Day

Movement Preparation:	8 Minutes

Perform 12 reps of the following exercises, then repeat. For single leg movements, perform 6 reps of each leg.

Rotator Cuff   Book Ends   Cat Stretch   Shoulder Girdle   Hurdler Walk   Cradlers

SUNDAY

Repeat Saturday or Rest

Pushing

PUSH-UP

Lay face down on floor and place hands shoulder-distance apart, flex your ankles, and come up on toes. Brace the abdominals then push away from floor. Fully extend your arms. Lower yourself toward floor so that your elbows are bent to 90 degrees. Be sure to be aware of your posture, keeping your head aligned with your spine and not sagging at the hips. If you cannot keep good form, begin doing the push-up on your knees.

TRI-DOG SAYS:
The push-up is not only an upper body exercise; it is very effective for strengthening the core. In addition, as in swimming, biking, and running, we are either pushing our body through resistance (water/air) or overcoming inertia (resistance to movement).

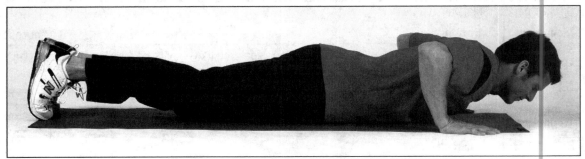

Pushing

HANDS ON THE PHYSIO-BALL

Begin kneeling in front of ball. Place your hands on the ball so that your fingertips are facing away from one another The placement of your hands on the ball is very important as this exercise can cause stress to your wrist. Draw your navel in. Push your toes into the floor while simultaneously contracting the quads, extending your arms, and lifting your hips. Slowly lower your chest toward ball. Do not allow your chest to bounce off the ball. Keep your movement under control.

TRI-DOG SAYS:
Doing the push-up with your hands on the ball is a great way to strengthen your shoulder girdle and prepare you for those sudden bumps on the road when biking! Place the ball against a wall when beginning if you need more stabilization.

Pushing

HANDS ON FLOOR/FEET ON BALL

Place your waist on the ball with your hands on the floor in front of you. Slowly walk with your hands, rolling the ball to it's appropriate position on your body. Keep your legs together. The further you walk your hands out, the lower the ball placement is on your legs, and the more challenging this exercise becomes. A good starting point for this exercise is with your knees on the ball. Keep your abs braced and do not allow your hips to sag. Slowly lower your chest toward the floor and return to starting position.

TRI-DOG SAYS:
An advanced push-up further challenges core stability and strength.

VARIATION

Pulling

FLEX ARM HANG

This exercise requires the use of a pull-up bar, Smith machine, or squat rack. If you don't have access to a gym, you can usually find monkey bars at a local school. A sturdy tree limb will also work. Hold the bar with your hands facing you. Bring your chin to the height of the bar. Hold as long as you can. Record your time. Lower yourself down slowly and repeat.

TRI-DOG SAYS:
Flex arm hangs are one of the best ways to increase your overall upper-body strength, which will lead to an increased level of endurance capability. Changing the hand grip so that your palms are facing away from you will increase the difficulty of this exercise.

Pulling

LAT PULL-DOWN

Sit with chest high and shoulders back. Hold bar so that your hands are shoulder-width apart with your palms facing away from you. First draw your shoulder blades down your back and then pull the bar down toward your upper chest. Elbows come toward the side of your ribs.

TRI-DOG SAYS:
Think of your hands as hooks so that you don't waste energy gripping the bar. Doing the pull-downs with your palms facing away from you (pronated) simulates the power stroke in swimming.

Pulling

PULL-UP

Place hands on bar shoulder-width apart with palms facing away from you. Do not wrap your thumbs around the bar. Come to a full hang with arms extended. In a controlled fashion, not swinging or jerking, pull your body up until chin comes over bar. Lower all the way down.

TRI-DOG SAYS:
If full pull-up is too difficult, continue working on the flex arm hang. Or do the pull-up eccentrically, which means executing only the lowering portion of the pull-up. Use a chair, start at top position, and slowly lower. Repeat. Be aware that lots of eccentric exercise can make you very sore.

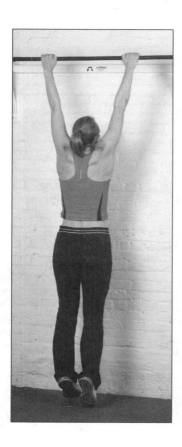

Squatting

WEIGHTED FRONT SQUAT

Stand with feet shoulder-width apart. Hold barbell or dumbbells at chest height. Keep toes facing forward with heels firmly on floor. Inhale before lowering. Press and lower hips back to the point where your thighs are parallel to the floor. Only lower your body to the point where you can keep the natural curve in your lower back. Keep your chest high. Slowly exhale and return to starting position. Knees should not move beyond the front of your toes.

TRI-DOG SAYS:
The weighted front squat is a safe way to load up the lumbar erectors (large back muscles) and build quad and glute strength. Strong back + strong glutes + strong quads = strong bike. If you have flexibility problems, I recommend you do the squat in what is known as a sumo position: feet shoulder-width or more apart with toes pointing to the side, like a ballerina. Doing the front squat in the sumo position will target more your inner thighs and hamstrings.

Squatting

STATIONARY LUNGE

We find the best way to properly set up for a stationary lunge is to begin by placing one knee on the floor with opposite foot placed in front of you. Flex the toe of the rear foot. Both front and back knees should be bent to 90 degrees. Keep your torso high, chest up, and shoulders back. Focus and contract the glute and the quadriceps of the forward leg. Press down on floor with the forward foot and come up to a standing position. The movement should be strictly vertical, focusing on strengthening the forward leg. Lower rear knee back down toward floor but not touching it.

 TRI-DOG SAYS:
For the development of hip power and stability in the lower body, perform the stationary lunges. Increase intensity by holding dumbbells in hand.

Be aware of the discrepancy between the strength of each leg. Add an extra set of repetitions on a weak side. Always work to remove discrepancies or strength imbalances.

Squatting

PRONE MANUAL HAMSTRINGS

Lay on the floor. Stack one hand on top of the other, and put your chin on hands. Bend legs at knees and cross ankles. Draw the outermost leg toward butt, giving resistance to the movement with the opposing leg. Vary both the velocity and the resistance of the reps. This exercise requires you to add or decrease resistance. Also, changing the angle in which you bring your heel to your butt will target different hamstring muscles.

TRI-DOG SAYS:
Strengthening the hamstrings is important in stabilizing the hips. Increasing stability in the hips and knees will translate into improved power output during all lower-body movements (aka pedal stroke, running stride).

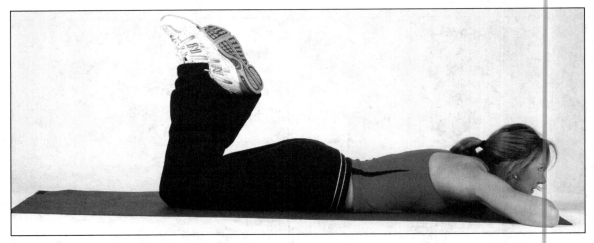

Lifting

DEADLIFT

Holding a dumbbell or barbell in your hands with arms extended, stand with feet hip-to-shoulder distance apart. Keep your chest high and your shoulders back. Inhale and brace your abs. Hinge forward at hips, not at the waist. Lower torso to 90 degrees at the hips while maintaining your neutral spine. Exhale slowly as you return to standing position. Keep knees slightly bent. Keep abs braced throughout the whole range of motion. You should feel this exercise in the back of your legs, butt, and lower back.

TRI-DOG SAYS:
The deadlift targets the much-needed strength of the body's posterior chain: the hamstrings, glutes, and lower back. These are important postural muscles for all three elements of a triathlon. This exercise must be done properly or it can hurt your back. I suggest beginning and practicing it with very light or no weight in front of a mirror. Focus on form and range of motion throughout the exercise.

Lifting

SINGLE LEG DEADLIFT

Stand with feet hip-distance apart. Stand on one leg with same side arm over head. Bend forward at hips, reaching hand toward floor as opposing leg extends behind you. Keep the natural curve of spine.

TRI-DOG SAYS:
Great for full-body control, flexibility, balance, and stabilization. Trains the back side of the body. Can be done with weight in hand as you become stronger or on unstable surface to increase challenge.

Lifting

SINGLE LEG SQUAT

Place one foot on box. Extend one leg in front. Inhale and brace your abs. Slowly lower until thighs are parallel. Keep the squatting leg's knee directly over second toe. Do not allow your knee to waffle or cave in. Maintain a natural curvature in your lower back. Exhale and return to starting position.

TRI-DOG SAYS:
Balance and stability drive strength. The single leg squat is the ideal exercise in keeping strength symmetry of your legs. A less strenuous method of learning the single leg squat is to place a bench or chair behind you and slowly lower your butt to the bench. This way you can control the depth of the squat, and as you become stronger you will be able to squat lower.

All About the Core

The deep postural muscles—the TVA, multifidus, pelvic floor, and diaphragm—together create intra-abdominal pressure (IAP) to stiffen the spine's structure so that the arms and legs have a stable foundation. Together they act like the body's natural weight belt. Imagine taking a long hot shower after your workout in the morning when someone flushes the toilet and you get dosed with ice cool water. You've just experienced IAP, which we will call 'bracing.'

The following are foundational exercises and must be embarked on first. If you are an experienced triathlete you may be tempted to charge directly into more advanced exercises. We don't recommend it. All other core exercises are based on how well you are able to execute the TVA ACTIVATION, BRACE and HIP BRIDGE.

Core

TVA ACTIVATION

Get on all fours, with hands directly under shoulders and knees directly under hips. Place a yoga belt or rope loosely around your waist. Maintain a neural spine. Take a natural breath in, allowing belly to expand and drop into the belt. Draw navel away from the belt as waist narrows. Continue breathing while holding your waist in. Hold for 10 seconds or as long as you can comfortably. Do this in front of mirror, being sure that there is absolutely no movement of the spine as you draw in your belly. Progression. A. Perform the TVA Activation on all fours. B. In a kneeling position. C. Perform it standing.

TRI-DOG SAYS:
TVA Activation is the foundation for building strong abs. The TVA is also known as the body's natural or organic weight belt. Keeping it strong will help you avoid lower back stress in all three sports.

Core

THE BRACE

Lay supine on floor, knees bent, and hands by thighs, palms up. Take a natural breath in, allowing belly to expand. Perform the TVA Activation, then a pelvis floor contraction. Hold for 10 seconds and repeat.

TRI-DOG SAYS:
Regardless of your training level the brace is an exercise that should be used to connect or reconnect to the core. Creating the "brace" means creating intra-abdominal pressure (IAP). IAP is what keeps the spine from crumbling when we pick a weighted object up or exert ourselves in any athletic or everyday movement. The pelvic floor lay between the anus and the scrotum in males and the vagina in women. To perform pelvis floor contraction, lay on your back on the floor. Imagine interrupting the flow of urination.

Core

HIP BRIDGE

Lay with back on floor. Bend knees to 90 degrees. Place hands by hips with palms facing the ceiling. The following successive movement will allow proper execution of this exercise:

A. Inhale, then draw belly button to spine.
B. Perform the TVA Activation.
C. Contract pelvis floor then clench your buttocks and lift your hips off the floor.
D. At the top end of this exercise, your knees, hips, and shoulders should be in a direct line.

TRI-DOG SAYS:
Perform this exercise in a slow and controlled fashion, 3:1:3 tempo. Strengthens and engages the core in conjunction with the hamstrings, glutes and lower back. Strengthens the glutes, and stretches the hip flexors. Great exercise for countering poor posture. If you have a job where you sit all day, then this exercise is your personal friend.

Core

SUPERMAN

Lay on floor, extend arms over head. Keep thumbs pointed up. Keep leg straight, contract abdominals, and lift both arms and legs off floor. Hold up to 60 seconds.

TRI-DOG SAYS:
These are exercises that strengthen the deep spinal muscles. These are the postural muscles needed to keep your torso upright and your spine healthy. It makes no sense to be able to do a 200-lb. deadlift if your back hurts every time you bend over to pick up a pencil.

Core

LATERAL BALL ROLL

Sitting on the apex of the physio-ball, walk down until your head and shoulders are comfortably supported on the ball. Be sure that your neck maintains it's natural curve. Knees, hips, and shoulders will be in a direct line if observed from the side. Your arms will be positioned out to the side, parallel to the height of the torso. Slowly crawl to one side while keeping the hips elevated. Avoid clocking moments. You should move strictly parallel. The supported shoulder will be pressing into the physio-ball with the opposing glute tightening and supporting.

TRI-DOG SAYS:
Allow glutes and hips to engage, along with the spine. This exercise is applicable to the triathlete because it develops body awareness and balance in response to our environment. As in all rotational sports, including the swimming component of triathlons, awareness of the glute and shoulder synergy is extremely important for power and stability.

TRIPOWER

Phase 2: Building

5

The basic principle of strength training is called 'overload.' There is an old legend of a farmer that decides to get stronger by lifting a baby calf every day. The theory is that as the calf gets bigger and weighs more, the farmer will become stronger as he lifts the calf every day—thus, someday he will be able to lift a cow. It's a good theory but of course it is flawed. (There will be a day when he will no longer be able to lift the calf because it becomes too large.)

We're not trying to make you lift a cow because we can't see how that would help you become a better triathlete. But we do want to place your musculoskeletal system under stress. You will do it by progressively increasing the weight used in an exercise. If properly done, the body will adapt to the stress and both the nervous and muscular systems become stronger. In Phase 2 we

focus on the development of the muscles know as 'primary movers.' The primary movers are the muscles responsible for the movements of your limbs.

It can require anywhere from 4 to 8 weeks in Phase 2 to achieve real strength gains, depending on an athlete's training background. But just as important is your body's neurological adaptation in Phase 2. This is where your mind and body come together. You will feel stronger because you are becoming more efficient at doing the exercises. The more efficient you are at performing a movement, the less energy you expend. Your body thus adapts to the stress as you develop higher muscle activation. The more muscle fibers you can activate, the more you can call on for help when you become exhausted.

Building Phase

Length: 3 Months

The Building Phase will be the most mentally challenging of all the phases. It requires dedication and consistency to stick with a strength program for an extended period of time. This is your chance to prove you can do it.

Increase the intensity of your workouts towards the middle to end of this phase. You should be challenging your body with progressively heavier weights. We suggest increasing the load every two weeks by 5% for your upper body and by 10-20% for your lower body. You have a number of reps and sets to be completed per exercise. Follow these recommendations, but realize the body will respond as it sees fit from week to week. Your recovery time on Monday/Wednesday/Friday will be vital, as your muscle tissue will be broken down during this phase more than the others. Hence, to help you recover at a faster rate after the challenging Building phase workouts, perform the myofascial release using the foam roller.

We do ask you to strictly adhere to the Tempo or speed prescribed per exercise. A 2/1/2 Tempo means each repetition would be 5 seconds in length, or three seconds on the pulling part of the exercise (raising a dumbbell/bodyweight/bungee), one on the top of the movement (holding the dumbbell/bodyweight/bungee), and two on the recovery part (lowering the dumbbell/bodyweight/ bungee). Complete the weekly schedule one week at a time, and evaluate your progress at the end of the week by using the Strength and Flexibility Assessments.

MONDAY/WEDNESDAY/FRIDAY

Corrective Strength Movements:	5 Minutes

Perform 20 second holds of the following exercises, then repeat. You should apply the corrective movements you most need based upon your self-administered assessments. We suggest performing the following sections together as their function relates:

Symptom	Area
poor upper body score	2 exercises each from Neck and Shoulders
poor back/lower body score	2 exercises each from Back and Lower Body

Core:	5 Minutes

Perform 20 repetitions or seconds of the following exercises, then repeat twice without pausing.

Prone Plank   Side Plank   Static Back Extension on Ball   Bent Knee Side Plank

Myofascial:	5 Minutes

Perform 45 seconds of the following movements. This should be the last piece of your workout.

IT Band   Adductors   Quadriceps   Piriformis   Rhomboids

TUESDAY/THURSDAY

Movement Preparation:					5 Minutes

Perform 10 reps of the following exercises, then repeat. For single leg movements, perform 5 reps of each leg.
  Cat Stretch   Hurdler Walk   Cradlers   Star

Building Strength Training Phase					30 minutes
Exercise	**Repetitions**	**Sets**	**Load**	**Rest**	**Tempo**
PUSH (1 of 3)					
Chest Press on Ball	10	2-3	75-85% Max	1 minute	2/1/2
Chest Flies on Ball	10	2-3	75-85% Max	1 minute	2/1/2
Bilateral Chest Press on Ball	10	2-3	75-85% Max	1 minute	2/1/2
PULL (1 of 3)					
Single Arm Standing Row	10	2-3	75-85% Max	1 minute	2/1/2
Single Arm Standing Row on One Leg	10	2-3	75-85% Max	1 minute	2/1/2
Pronated Grip Pull-Ups	Perform until failure		Bodyweight	1 minute	2/1/2
SQUAT (2 of 4)					
Front Squat	10	2-3	75-85% Max	1 minute	2/1/2
Single Leg Step-Up	10 per leg	2-3	75-85% Max	1 minute	2/1/2
Static Single Leg Lunge with Arms Raised	10 per leg	2-3	80-85% Max	1 minute	2/1/2
Supine Hamstring Curl on Ball	10 per leg	2-3	Bodyweight	1 minute	2/1/2
LIFT (1 of 2)					
Deadlift	10	2-3	75-85% Max	1 minute	2/1/2
Single Leg Deadlift	10 per leg	2-3	75-85% Max	1 minute	2/1/2

SATURDAY

Sport Specific Skill Day

Movement Preparation:	8 Minutes

Perform 12 reps of the following exercises, then repeat. For single leg movements, perform 6 reps of each leg.
  Cat Stretch   Hurdler Walk   Star   Elbow Lunges
    Cradlers (alternate with variations: Static Single Leg, Walking Pulls, Dynamic Skips)

SUNDAY

Repeat Saturday or Rest

Pushing

DUMBBELL CHEST PRESS ON PHYSIO-BALL

Sit on apex of ball with dumbbells on thighs. Walk your feet out so that you are in a bridge position on the ball. Knees, hips, and shoulders should be in a direct line, no sagging at the hips. Keep your glutes engaged. Make sure that your neck is positioned on the ball so that it maintains its natural curve. Begin by pressing the dumbbells above your chest. The dumbbells should now be aligned with your nipple line of your chest with your palms facing down toward the feet. Slowly lower the dumbells until your upper arms are at a 90-degree angle. Be sure the weights stay directly in line over the elbow throughout the range of motion. Return the dumbells to starting position.

TRI-DOG SAYS:
Doing chest presses on the ball will not only target your chest but also engage your abs and your extensor chain—the lower back, glutes, hamstrings—giving you a big bang for one exercise. Because the feet are on the floor and used to stabilize you, this exercise has a greater transference for biking and running, as opposed to a chest press on a machine.

Pushing

DUMBBELL FLY ON PHYSIO-BALL

Sit on apex of ball with dumbbells on thighs. Walk feet out so that you are in a bridge position on the ball. Knees, hips, and shoulders should be in a direct line, no sagging at the hips. Keep your glutes engaged. Make sure that your neck is positioned on the ball so that it maintains its natural curve. Begin by pressing the dumbbells above your chest, with the palms facing each other and a slight bend in the elbows. Slowly lower the dumbbells until the upper arms are near parallel to the floor. You should never lower the weight to a level where you cannot see them in your peripheral vision. Slowly return the dumbells to starting position and avoid clinking the dumbbells together.

TRI-DOG SAYS:
Dumbbell flies will target the center portion of the chest in addition to the biceps. Strengthening the biceps adds stability to the shoulder joint and aids in preventing bicep tendonitis.

Pushing

BILATERAL DUMBBELL PRESS ON PHYSIO-BALL

Sit on apex of ball with dumbbells on thighs. Walk feet out so that you are in a bridge position on the ball. Knees, hips, and shoulders should be in a direct line, no sagging at the hips. Keep your glutes engaged. Make sure that your neck is positioned on the ball so that it maintains its natural curve. Begin by pressing both dumbbells over your chest. With both dumbbells now over your chest, begin by lowering one dumbbell. Keeping one dumbbell low and one dumbbell high, alternate the position of the dumbbells with simultaneous movement. Be sure the weights stay directly in line over the elbows throughout the whole of motion. Return the dumbbells to starting position.

TRI-DOG SAYS:
Bilateral dumbbell presses are excellent for activating the core while enhancing stability and balance throughout the body.

UNILATERAL, or single limb, exercises for the triathlete are superior to BILATERAL. Swimming, biking, and running are dominated by coordinated single-limb movements. Unilateral exercises will help balance strength development from right and left side, equating the amount of strength endurance and power delivery on either side.

Pulling

ONE ARM STANDING ROW

Standing with feet in a staggered lunge position, one foot in front of the other, hold a dumbbell in one hand on the side of the trailing leg. Slightly bend your knees, with the front knee more bent. Flex forward at the hip, not the waist, being careful not to round at the back. Keep abdominals engaged. Let dumbell hang by side. Keep hand cuffed but do not squeeze the weight. Begin by drawing your shoulder blade back then follow by pulling your elbow back along the ribcage. Lower weight to starting position.

 TRI-DOG SAYS:
Strengthens the back, torso, and core. Being strong in a forward flexed position will improve endurance and posture on bike.

Pulling

ONE ARM STANDING ROW, ONE HAND ON BALL

Stand with feet hip-distance apart in front of the ball. Hold dumbbell in one hand and place finger tips of other hand on ball. Draw belly tight and bend from hips, not the waist. Lift the leg that is in front of ball directly behind you until your leg is parallel to floor. Be sure to keep your hips squared. Do not round over the back. Bend the knee of the standing leg slightly. Pull weight so that elbow sides are next to the ribcage. Return to starting position. We highly recommend that you attempt this exercise first with no or little weight in your hand.

TRI-DOG SAYS:
A multifaceted exercise that will improve strength, stability, and balance.

Pulling

PULL-UP WITH PRONATED GRIP

Hold the bar with your palms facing away from you at shoulder-distance apart. Allow yourself to hang with arms fully extended. Imagine your hands as hooks so that you do not waste energy squeezing the bar. Then pull your chest up until chin is over bar. Slowly return to starting position. Do not allow your body to swing or use momentum when performing pull-ups. If you find the pull-up too advanced, you can begin with the flex arm hang. Or you can use a chair to stand up on so that you start the pull-up in the up position and slowly lower yourself down. Stand back on chair and repeat. Avoid wrapping your thumbs around the bar, as this will pre-fatigue your forearm.

TRI-DOG SAYS:
Pull-ups are to the upper body what squats are to the lower body. If you only had one exercise you could do for your upper body, the pull-up would be my choice.

Squatting

FRONT SQUAT WITH WEIGHT

Keep feet at hip-to shoulder-distance apart with toes pointing forward. Hold weight in hands at shoulder height. Keep chest high and your spine in neutral position. Keep abdominals firmly braced. Inhale, then slowly lower your hips back as though you're going to sit in a chair. Lower them until back of thighs are parallel to floor. Knees should be directly aligned with toes. Heels should not come off floor. Keeping your weight firmly on your heels and lifting your toes in your shoes will help keep your hips back. Exhale as you begin your upward movement by firmly pressing your heels into the ground and slowly returning to starting position.

TRI-DOG SAYS:
The front squat is an excellent exercise for the triathlete. By placing the weight in front of your body during a squat it creates heavy engagement of the core and back musculature, thus strengthening the legs and enhancing posture.

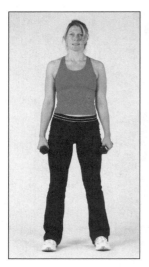

VARIATION

Squatting

SINGLE LEG STEP-UP WITH DUMBBELL

Place one foot firmly on step. Be sure that the height is not so high that your knee is higher than your hips. The knee should be bent at 90 degrees or less if you have knee issues. Hold dumbbells in hands. Step up on bench, touching the step with the opposing foot, then return to starting position. Keep your chest high and your shoulders back throughout the whole exercise. Focus on feeling the exertion in the quadriceps and glute of the lead leg. Avoid assisting the step up by bouncing off the floor with the foot of the trailing leg. Make it a controlled movement.

TRI-DOG SAYS:
Unilateral exercise such as the single leg step-up will help balance your strength between the left and right leg. The more balanced you are, the more even distribution of power you can apply on the road when running and on the pedals when biking.

Squatting

SINGLE LEG LUNGE WITH BOX AND WEIGHT OVERHEAD

In a staggered lunge position with one foot in front of the other, place the toes of the trailing leg behind on a bench. The bench can be anywhere from ankle to knee height. Hold the weights in hand and extend the arms overhead. Keep the abs braced and bend the front knee. This will place stress on the thigh muscles of forward leg while providing a stretch on the trailing leg's thigh and hip flexor. Keep knee pointed over first two toes—do not allow it to wobble. By holding the weight overhead it enhances shoulder stability and trunk strength.

TRI-DOG SAYS:
This exercise requires stability and balance. It enhances shoulder girdle and core strength, strengthening through movements, not muscle isolation.

Squatting

HAMSTRING CURL SUPINE ON PHYSIO-BALL

Lay supine face-up on floor and place your hands by thighs with palms facing the sky. Place your ankles on top of ball. Draw belly tight, then engage your glutes and slowly lift your hips off the floor. Your hips, knees, and ankles should be in a direct line at the end point of the lift. Then with your ankles, roll the ball toward your glutes, keeping your hips elevated. Slowly straighten your legs, rolling the ball back, then lower the hips to the floor. Avoid shifting your hips while maintaining control of the ball.

TRI-DOG SAYS:
Excellent functional exercise for the posterior chain, hams, glutes, and lower back. These are the muscles that assist in maintaining correct posture and preventing lower back pain.

Lifting

SINGLE LEG DEADLIFT WITH WEIGHT

Stand with feet hip-distance apart. Extend one arm over your head with dumbbell in hand. Bend the standing leg's knee and lift the opposite foot off floor. Bend at the hips and reach your hand directly toward floor. At the same time, extend the same-side leg behind you. Return to starting position. Avoid using momentum and concentrate on your core. Practice this exercise first with no dumbbell in hands.

TRI-DOG SAYS:
Single leg deadlift increases core strength, stability, balance, and hip strength.

Core

PRONE PLANK

Lay on stomach, and place elbows directly under shoulder. Lift your hips off floor and come up on toes. Press palms together and make the intention to pull the elbows apart. Keep head, shoulders, and hips in a direct line. Brace abdominals tightly. Breathe, and as you exhale, envision your waist narrowing. Hold for at least 60 seconds.

TRI-DOG SAYS:
Pushing the palms together and elbows apart relaxes the chest and superficial ab muscles, thus engaging the deeper abdominal muscles.

Core

SIDE PLANK

Lay on side with legs stacked one on top of the other. Place supporting elbow directly under shoulder and opposing arm on side. Lift hips off floor. Keep shoulders, hips, and legs in a straight line. You will feel the burn on the side of the waist closest to floor. No sagging of hips.

TRI-DOG SAYS:
The side plank will strengthen the internal oblique. The internal oblique is a major stabilizer of the lower back.

Core

STATIC BACK EXTENSION ON PHYSIO-BALL

With knees on floor, place the front of your hips on ball. Be sure placement of ball does not impede breathing. Put hands on floor. Anchor heels on a bench or rail behind you. Lift hands off floor and place arms down by thigh, rotate palms to floor, and squeeze shoulder blades together. Avoid hyperextending the neck. Keep torso parallel to floor. Hold at least 60 seconds.

TRI-DOG SAYS:
The static back extension engages and strengthens the posterior extensors, hamstrings, glutes, and lower back. If you feel back strain during long bikerides or runs, this exercise is what you need to alleviate the strain. It is also a great posture exercise.

Core

BENT KNEE SIDE PLANK

Lay on side with legs stacked. Place bottom elbow directly under shoulder. Bend the bottom leg at the knee, keeping top leg straight. Elevate hip off floor and extend and hold top leg parallel to floor. This exercise should be performed at least twice on each side for proper effect. Hold for 30 seconds per side then alternate.

TRI-DOG SAYS:
The bent knee side plank strengthens the often-ignored side of the glutes. The glute medius is a major stabilizer of the pelvis. A stable pelvis keeps hips from swaying side-to-side and makes leg movements more efficient.

Phase 3: Power

6

In Phase 3, you will begin to develop power, defined as the rate at which work is done. In this phase, you will recruit fast twitch muscle fibers that will accomplish a large amount of work very quickly. You remember them—the chickens, those muscle fibers that are powerful but fatigue quickly.

Now, you may ask why you need fast twitch muscle fibers in a sport that is predominately slow twitch. It's the use-it-or-lose-it theory. If you never activate your fast twitch muscle fibers, don't expect them to come to your assistance if you need extra stroke power to get out of a side current when swimming, when you need extra power to bike up a hill, or if you decide to sprint to the finish line. Research has demonstrated that there is a fast-to-slow fiber transformation. This means with training, your fast twitch can become slow twitch. Throughout Phase 3 you will also discover that the exercises have become more sports-specific, preparing you for your tri season.

Power Phase

Length: 2 Months

The Power Phase leads directly up to your racing season. During this period, your body will begin to transfer the strength gains made during the building phase, into explosive athletic movements simple enough for the inexperienced triathlete.

Increase the intensity of your workouts towards the end of this phase. This intensity is important, but so is the recovery between your sets. Always start these power movements from the ground up. This means you should push from the part/s of your body that are in contact with the ground, which gives you a feeling of support upon take off, and an enhanced aware-ness of your body when you return to your starting position.

Be sure to strictly adhere to the Tempo. A 1/0/1 Tempo means each repetition would be 2 seconds in length, or one second on the power part of the exercise (raising a dumbbell/bodyweight/bungee), then going directly into a one second recovery (lower-ing the dumbbell/bodyweight/bungee), with no pause at the top of the movement.

Complete the weekly schedule one week at a time, and evaluate your progress at the end of the week by using the Strength and Flexibility Assessments.

MONDAY/WEDNESDAY/FRIDAY	
Corrective Strength Movements:	**5 Minutes**
Perform 20 second holds of the following exercises, then repeat. You should apply the corrective movements you most need based upon your self-administered assessments. We suggest performing the following sections together as their function relates:	

Symptom	Area
poor upper body score	Neck/Shoulders/Chest stretches
poor mid/lower back score	Lower Back/Hamstring/Calf stretches
poor hip/lower body score	Glutes/Hip Flexors/IT-Band/Quad stretches

Core:	**5 Minutes**
Perform 10 repetitions or seconds of the following exercises, then repeat twice without pausing.	

Physioball Crunch	Extended Crunch on Ball	Inter-Oblique Crunch on Ball
Dynamic Back on Ball	Lower Abs	

Myofascial:	**5 Minutes**
Perform 45 seconds of the following movements. This should be the last piece of your workout.	

IT Band	Adductors	Quadriceps	Piriformis	Lats

TUESDAY/THURSDAY

Movement Preparation:	5 Minutes

Perform 10 reps of the following exercises, then repeat. For single leg movements, perform 5 reps of each leg.

Star   Elbow Lunges   Hands under Toes/Sumo Combo   Carioca

Power Strength Training Phase					30 minutes
Exercise	Repetitions	Sets	Load	Rest	Tempo
PUSH (All) Plyo Push-Ups	10	1-3	Bodyweight	1 minute	1/0/1

PULL (All)
  Dumbbell Alternating
    Rows
	10	1-3	80-90% Max	1 minute	1/0/1

Standing Straight Arm Pulldown	10	1-3	80-90% Max	1 minute	1/0/1
SQUAT (1 of 2) 2 Foot Box Jump	10-15	1-3	Bodyweight	2> minutes	1/0/1
2 Foot Box Jump, Single Foot Landing	10-15	1-3	Bodyweight	2> minutes	1/0/1
LIFT (All) Squat and Press	15	1-3	75-90% Max	2> minutes	1/0/1

SATURDAY

Sport Specific Skill Day

(Optional) Movement Preparation:	8 Minutes

Perform 12 reps of the following exercises, then repeat. For single leg movements, perform 6 reps of each leg.

Star   Elbow Lunges   Hands under Toes/Sumo Combo   Carioca

Walking Single Leg Hamstring Stretch Backwards   Ballistic Hamstring Kick

SUNDAY

Repeat Saturday or Rest

Pushing

PLYO PUSH-UP

Place your hands on floor shoulder-width apart. Flex your ankles and come up on your toes with legs hip- to shoulder-width apart. Lower chest toward floor until elbows are flexed at 90 degrees. Contract your chest muscles and push explosively off floor. You should generate enough power so that your hands come off the floor. Prior to making contact again with the floor, slightly flex your elbows as this will ready your chest to slow the upper body down very quickly. Catch your weight with your hands as you return to floor, lower, and repeat. Brace your abs throughout this exercise.

TRI-DOG SAYS:
Improves core stability and explosive power of the chest, shoulders, and arms. Plyos can be for everyone. The above are advanced. To decrease intensity, these push-ups can be done against a wall, on a bench, or on your knees.

Pulling

ALTERNATING BENT-OVER ONE ARM ROW

Stand with feet shoulder-width apart, chest up, and shoulders back. Keep knees slightly bent. Hold dumbbell in one hand and bend forward at your hips. Keep head aligned with your spine. Do not round your back—be sure to maintain a neutral spine. Keep abdominal muscles braced. Draw shoulder blades back and then pull weight backward, allowing your elbow to lead the way past the ribcage. Lower dumbbell and place it on the floor. Pick up the dumbbell with your opposing hand and pull it back so that your elbow slides past the ribcage. If you do not have the flexibility to maintain a neutral spine when lowering or picking up the dumbbell, use a crate or box to provide a higher starting position.

TRI-DOG SAYS:
Holding this bent-over position properly while performing an alternating row helps build muscular endurance in the spinal muscles. Increased muscular endurance enhances a neutral spine, which leads to proper posture, improved breathing efficiency, and strengthening of the obliques, ultimately allowing the triathlete to push through training more effectively.

Pulling

STANDING CABLE/BUNGEE STRAIGHT ARM CROSS PULLDOWN

Cable or bungee should be anchored high enough so that when you when initiate this exercise, your hands are over your head. Hold the cable/bungee with both hands, palms down. Keep arms straight. Feet should be shoulder-distance apart, knees slightly bent, abdominals braced. Bending forward at hips, initiate the pull of the cable by first drawing your shoulder blades then pulling cable down until your arms come down to the side. Return to upright position with a slow controlled movement. Head should be positioned forward throughout the entire movement.

TRI-DOG SAYS:
Develops power throughout the entire swim stroke by providing resistance on the pulling and recovery portions of the stroke cycle.

Squatting

TWO FOOT BOX JUMP

Stand with feet shoulder-distance apart. Keep chest high, shoulders back, and abs braced. Sit your hips back and jump off a platform or other stable surface. Flex hips before landing on both feet. Decelerate your body weight as quickly as possible upon landing, squat, and quickly jump again. You can begin this exercise without a platform, jumping on a flat surface and slowly incorporating a low platform or box. When you can comfortably execute a set, increase height of platform 3 to 6 inches.

TRI-DOG SAYS:
Improves balance and explosive power in the hips and legs. For the triathlete who has balance or strength issues, jumping down from a box will decrease shearing force on joints and develop explosive power, via the stretch-shortening cycle, while increasing confidence in executing explosive movements.

Squatting

TWO FOOT BOX JUMP ALTERNATIVE

Stand with feet shoulder-distance apart. Keep chest high, shoulders back, and abs braced. Sit your hips back and jump off platform. Flex hips before landing on both feet. Decelerate as quickly as possible upon landing, squat, and jump, pushing off both feet, and landing on other platform with one foot, hold, and stabilize briefly.

TRI-DOG SAYS:
Develops equal leg power. Improves balance and explosive power to hips and legs. Also increases core strength and body control.

Lifting

SINGLE LEG BOX JUMP

Stand with your feet together about a foot away from a box. Inhale and brace your abs. Swing your arms to gain the momentum needed to jump up on the box. Land on one food. Resume the starting position and repeat, landing on opposite foot.

TRI-DOG SAYS:
By landing on one foot, you are building up your balance and stability. For a more difficult exercise, try attempting this without swinging your arms.

Lifting

DUMBBELL SQUAT CURL AND PRESS

Stand with feet shoulder-width apart. Hold dumbbells by your side with both hands. Bend your elbow and curl the dumbbells to your shoulders. Holding the dumbbells at shoulder height, drop down into a squat, pressing your hips back as though you're sitting in a chair. Keep the chest high and maintain the neutral spine position. Keep heels pressed to floor and lift toes in shoes. Lower hips until thighs are parallel to floor. As you drive your hip up to starting position, push the dumbbells explosively up and above your shoulders. Keep driving the heels into the ground, leading the body into a vertical direction. Return to starting position and repeat.

TRI-DOG SAYS:
Strengthen the glutes, quads, shoulders, and upper back. The sport of triathlon is a full-body dynamic movement calling on explosive muscular contractions as you sprint and climb. Use that mindset in this movement.

Core

PHYSIO-BALL CRUNCH

Sit on ball and walk feet forward until lower back is firmly supported on the ball. Begin with hands behind head. Extend torso as far back as possible, getting a stretch of the abdominals. Contract the abdominals and lift shoulder blades off ball. Increase intensity by holding a weight on chest. Do not extend head back if it makes you dizzy.

TRI-DOG SAYS:
The biggest benefit of doing a crunch on a physio-ball is that the torso can go to extension, which cannot be done with a crunch on the floor. This crunch strengthens primarily the rectus abdominal, which stabilizes the spine when the trunk is in extension.

Core

EXTENDED CRUNCH ON PHYSIO-BALL

Sit on ball and walk feet forward until lower back is firmly on ball. Hold weights in hand. Extend arms over chest. Extend torso backward over ball then contract abdominals, pressing the weight of one hand up and across the body. Return to original position and lift up, pressing opposing hand across body.

TRI-DOG SAYS:
If you feel stress behind the head, drop one weight and support head. The external oblique is primarily responsible for shoulder-to-hip rotation.

Core

INTER-OBLIQUE CRUNCH ON PHYSIO-BALL

Sit slightly to the side of the apex of ball. Keep center leg bent at 90 degrees. Extend opposite leg out to side with foot anchored to wall. Begin holding hands across chest. Flex laterally to side until opposing shoulder touches ball then return to original position. Increase intensity of exercise by holding a weight across chest

TRI-DOG SAYS:
Be sure the movement stays through a frontal plane, so that your shoulders do not rotate.

Core

DYNAMIC BACK EXTENSION ON PHYSIO-BALL

Place hips on ball. Anchor heels on bench or rail. Keep legs straight. Hold weight across chest. Lower trunk toward floor and return to horizontal position.

TRI-DOG SAYS:
The dynamic back extension strengthens the erector back muscles, the primary muscles that keep the trunk erect.

Core

LOWER ABS

Lay on your back with knees bent, and feet flat on floor. Place hands by side with palms facing up. Hold medicine ball between thighs. Press your lower back to the floor. Brace your abs and draw your knees to the chest. Slowly lower your feet until your toes touch the floor. If you cannot keep your lower back firmly on the floor while lowering your feet, modify range of motion of the exercise. Focus on the abdominals directly above your pubic bone.

TRI-DOG SAYS:
Triathletes tend to have overactive hip flexors that will overpower the easily fatigued lower abdominal muscles. By performing this exercise correctly, the lower abdominals will not only stabilize the lower back, but help in preventing lower cross syndrome.

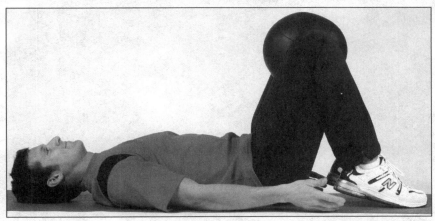

TRIPOWER

Phase 4: Maintenance

7

Maintenance means to keep in existence the conditioning you have created during the previous phases. In other words: Don't discontinue strength training once the season has started. To quote Dr. Tubor Bompa, "Staying up is always easier than falling down and attempting to get on one's feet." You want to make sure you maintain a strong and stable base.

In Phase 4 the goal is to maintain your muscular strength and continue to train and adapt your coping powers and ability to push through fatigue. You will notice that the exercises are performed by time, not reps. The resistance levels are low and the repetitions are high. The primary manipulation of the intensity of this phase is the rest period. Highly trained triathletes will be able to go from one exercise to another with little rest. Beginners will be able to adjust according to their fitness level.

Maintenance Phase

Length: 4-6 Months

It may appear as if this phase is long, however, that's deceptive. It will run through your entire racing season. Your body can easily plateau during this season, so it's best to make sure the intensity of your workouts peaks halfway between races. You can do this by simply altering the tension, length, numbers of sets, or time of rest between sets.

In the Maintenance Phase, your exercises are completed using only bungee or body weight resistance. You will be working your muscles according to the clock rather than a number of repetitions. To manipulate resistance, try moving your body further away from the point where the bungee is attached, or using a heavier bungee. Bungees are typically color-coded according to their level of resistance, darker increased resistance and lighter color less resistance.

Be sure to strictly adhere to the Tempo. A 1/0/1 Tempo means each repetition would be 2 seconds in length, or one second on the power part of the exercise (raising a dumbbell/bodyweight/bungee), then going directly into a one second recovery (lowering the dumbbell/bodyweight/bungee), with no pause at the top of the movement.

Complete the weekly schedule one week at a time, and evaluate your progress at the end of the week by using the Strength and Flexibility Assessments.

MONDAY/WEDNESDAY/FRIDAY

Corrective Strength Movements: 5 Minutes

Perform 20 second holds of the following exercises, then repeat. You should apply the corrective movements you most need based upon your self-administered assessments. We suggest performing the following sections together as their function relates:

Symptom	Area
poor upper body score	2 exercises each from Neck and Shoulders
poor back/lower body score	2 exercises each from Back and Lower Body

Core: 5 Minutes

Perform 10 repetitions or seconds of the following exercises, then repeat twice without pausing.

Supine Russian Twist with Medicine Ball   Standing Medicine Ball Rotations

Standing Horizontal Rotations   Downward and Upward Ax Chops

Myofascial: 5 Minutes

Perform 45 seconds of the following movements. This should be the last piece of your workout.

Calves   Hamstrings   Latisimus Dorsi   IT Band   Adductors   Rhomboids

TUESDAY/THURSDAY

Movement Preparation:					5 Minutes

Perform 10 reps of the following exercises, then repeat. For single leg movements, perform 5 reps of each leg.
   Rotator Cuff   Cat Stretch   Supine/Prone Leg Swings   Hands under Toes/Sumo Combo

Maintenance Strength Training Phase					30 minutes
Exercise	Time	Sets	Resistance	Rest	Tempo
PUSH (1 of 2)					
Chest Press with Band	30 seconds to 3 minutes	1-3	Light to heavy	Less than 1 minute	1/0/1
Staggered Stance Lunge Press	30 seconds to 3 minutes	1-3	Light to heavy	Less than 1 minute	1/0/1
PULL (1 of 2)					
Straight Arm Pulldown	30 seconds to 3 minutes	1-3	Light to heavy	Less than 1 minute	1/0/1
Kneeling Cable Pull and Push	30 seconds to 3 minutes	1-3	Light to heavy	Less than 1 minute	1/0/1
SQUAT (2 of 3)					
Squat and Pull	30 seconds to 3 minutes	1-3	Light to heavy	Less than 1 minute	1/0/1
Single Leg Step-Up with Knee Drive	30 seconds to 3 minutes	1-3	Bodyweight	Less than 1 minute	1/0/1
Lunge Walk with Toe Raises	30 seconds to 3 minutes	1-3	Bodyweight	Less than 1 minute	1/0/1
LIFT (1 of 2)					
Lateral Bungee Squat	30 seconds to 3 minutes	1-3	Light to heavy	Less than 1 minute	1/0/1
Cable Bungee Squat with Upright Row	30 seconds to 3 minutes	1-3	Light to heavy	Less than 1 minute	1/0/1

SATURDAY

Sport Specific Skill Day

Movement Preparation:					8 Minutes

Perform 12 reps of the following exercises, then repeat. For single leg movements, perform 6 reps of each leg.

   Rotator Cuff   Cat Stretch   Rotational Trunk Movements in Place
   Supine/Prone Leg Swings   Elbow Lunges   Hands under Toes/Sumo Combo

SUNDAY

Repeat Saturday or Rest

Pushing

CHEST PRESS BUNGEE

Anchor bungee at chest height. Stand in a staggered lunge position with one foot in front of the other. Hold bungee with palms turned down toward floor. Be sure that your hands, wrist, elbow, chest, bungee, and shoulders are in a direct line. Begin the chest press with your elbows bent to 90 degrees. Draw shoulder blades back. Avoid rounding the shoulders forward when pressing bungee forward.

TRI-DOG SAYS:
Strong chest muscles are part of the muscle group that contributes to the swimming stroke. Standing exercises are also more functional and transfer better to sports performance.

Pushing

STANDING STAGGERED LUNGE CHEST PRESS

Anchor bungee at chest height. Stand with feet together. Hold bungee with hands turn down. Hands, wrist, elbow, chest, bungee, and shoulders are in a direct line. Press the bungee away and step forward into a lunge. Front knee is flexed at 90 degrees. Bend back knee toward floor. Do not let rear knee hit the floor. Return to starting position. Repeat with the opposite leg.

TRI-DOG SAYS:
Get your heart pumping while engaging the chest, shoulder, arms, back, and legs. Total body exercise.

Pulling

STRAIGHT ARM PULL-DOWN

Anchor bungee above head height so that arms are over head. Hold bungee with both hands, palms down. Keep feet shoulder-distance apart, and knees slightly bent. Bend slightly forward at hips. Draw shoulder blades down and pull bungee down past thighs. Keep arms straight. Return arms to overhead position. Can be done either bilateral or unilateral.

 TRI-DOG SAYS:
Strengthens the power portion of the swim stroke.

Pulling

STANDING CABLE/MEDICINE BALL PULL/PUSH

You can use cable, bungee, medicine ball, or even a dumbbell to perform this exercise. Have cable or bungee attached low. Rotate body and point feet toward medicine ball, bend at hips and knees, keeping neutral spine. Hold medicine ball with both hands and pull it toward your chest. Rotate your torso and feet toward opposite side while pushing bungee overhead.

TRI-DOG SAYS:
Strengthens the upper back, chest, shoulders, and legs. Improves shoulder-to-hip rotational ability.

Pulling

KNEELING CABLE PULL AND PUSH

Kneel on one knee with opposing leg extended to side, perpendicular to cable. Place towel or mat under knee. Hold cable with both hands, and rotate chest toward cable. Pull cable toward you while turning shoulders and continue rotating shoulders and push it away. This exercise can also be performed with a dumbbell or a medicine ball.

TRI-DOG SAYS:
The kneeling cable push and pull removes the lower body from the exercise, making it a more upper body–dominate exercise.

Squatting

SQUAT AND PULL

Hold cable or band in hands. Stand with feet shoulder-width apart, chest high, and shoulders back. Extend arms in front of you then lower hips until thighs are parallel to floor. As you stand, draw shoulder blades back and pull cable/band backward, letting both elbows slide past ribcage. Keep abdominals engaged. Pinch shoulders back at the top when you stand. Keep heels firmly on floor; lifting toes in shoes will help you do this.

TRI-DOG SAYS:
Squat and pull is a multifunctional exercise involving ground contact using multiple planes of motion and stabilization.

Squatting

SINGLE LEG LUNGE WITH BUNGEE

Anchor cable at chest height. Extend arm in front of chest. Stand in a staggered lunge position, one foot in front of the other. As you lower your trailing knee toward the floor, pull cable back. Draw the shoulders back and pull the elbows past the ribcage. As you stand, extend arms in front. Trailing knee should not bounce off the floor. Keep the focus on the forward leg, glute, and thigh.

TRI-DOG SAYS:
Single leg lunge will make you aware of muscular imbalances between legs.

Squatting

ONE FOOT STEP-UP

Place one foot on step anywhere from 6 to 12 inches in height. Lean forward and step up, bringing your opposing knee to hip height. Return foot to floor and repeat with same leg. Repeat as quickly as possible for timed intervals of 15 to 30+ seconds. Use opposing arm-leg movement. Improves running form and leg strength for biking.

 TRI-DOG SAYS:
Do not continue exercise after form breaks down or you will be teaching yourself poor movement patterns.

Squatting

LUNGE WALK WITH TOES RAISED

Begin with feet hip-distance apart. Stand with perfect posture. Step forward with one leg. The lead leg should form a 90-degree angle. The trail knee should not hit the floor. Push off floor with lead leg and come up on toes as the trailing leg swings forward to the lunge.

TRI-DOG SAYS:
Strengthen the full kinetic chain from ankle to hip. It will include the often ignored foot extension, which is the drive off road when running.

Lifting

LATERAL SQUAT WITH CABLE AND DOUBLE ARMS

Stand with feet shoulder-width or wider apart. Anchor bungee at floor level. Hold bungee with both hands in an over-grip position. Keep shoulders back and press heels firmly on the floor. Bend one knee deeply and hold the bungee on the outside of the leg. Press firmly with the same leg to the lateral side. Bend the opposite knee and bring the bungee to the outside of the opposing leg. This will work your inner thigh and glute muscles. Can also be done with medicine ball.

 TRI-DOG SAYS:
Lateral movements are necessary for keeping hip stability but are often ignored. Be sure to maintain the natural curve of your back during the whole range of the squat.

Lifting

CABLE SQUAT WITH UPRIGHT ROW

Stand with feet shoulder-width apart. Anchor bungee low. Stand upright and hold bungee in hands with extended arms. Drop hips back to a seated position. As you stand, pull your elbows high.

TRI-DOG SAYS:
Strengthens the legs, glutes, upper back, and shoulders.

Core

SUPINE RUSSIAN TWIST WITH MEDICINE BALL

Sit on apex of physio-ball and walk down to a bridge position. Extend arms in front of chest holding medicine ball. Press hands together or hold weight between hands. Rotate trunk until arms are parallel to floor. Keep hips high through full range of motion, allowing feet to rotate.

TRI-DOG SAYS:
The Russian twist with weight in hands will strengthen and increase flexibility of the waist, hips, and glutes.

Core

STANDING MEDICINE BALL ROTATION

Stand with feet shoulder-width apart and knees slightly bent. Hold weight or medicine ball in front of chest with arms extended. Keep hips fixed in a forward position and rotate ball/weight 180 degrees. Bend knees; hold ball/weight on the outside of knee. Stand and rotate ball/weight over opposite shoulder. Bend knees, lowering weight between legs. Keep chest high and maintain neutral spine. Stand and lift ball/weight over head.

TRI-DOG SAYS:
The medicine ball rotation warms up the body in all ranges of motion, flexion, extension, and rotation.

Core

STANDING HORIZONTAL ROTATION

Anchor bungee or cable at chest level. Stand with feet shoulder-width apart. Keep knees slightly bent. Draw belly tight. Rotate shoulders toward where bungee/cable is anchored then to opposite side. Keep head facing forward.

TRI-DOG SAYS:
Strengthen internal and external obliques and the side of your waist. Improves hip-to-shoulder rotation.

Core

DOWNWARD AX CHOPS

Anchor bungee/cable high. Stand with feet shoulder-width apart. Keep knees slightly bent. Draw belly tight. Rotate shoulders toward where bungee/cable is anchored, then drop hips back, keep a straight back, and draw bungee/cable to the outside of the opposite knee. Allow trailing foot to rotate inward.

TRI-DOG SAYS:
Begin slowly and increase velocity.

Core

UPWARD AX CHOPS

Anchor bungee/cable low. Stand with feet shoulder-width apart. Keep knees slight bent. Draw belly tight. Drop hips back and low in seated position. Rotate shoulder toward anchored position, then come to standing position while rotating shoulders to opposing side. Keep a straight back with arms extended. Allow trailing foot to rotate inward.

 TRI-DOG SAYS:
Begin slowly and increase velocity.

TRIPOWER

Fixing the Weak Spots

8

Remember the old saying "You are only as strong as your weakest link?" This section will help you address your weak link. Let's take a walk down injury-prevention lane. We have a strong female triathlete who does all the right things, including watching her nutrition, stretching consistently, and following a progressive strength-training regiment. She's getting older, and her out-of-date training program has not aged with her. This triathlete has not recognized that she also needs to age her strength-training program because an older body has different needs.

Triathletes commonly develop imbalances through repetitive stress because most of our training and racing time is spent moving through the same plane of movement: forward. You shouldn't work on increasing your running to the point where you ignore working your lateral muscles up your side, as they will help prevent injuries. We don't expect you to know all the muscle groups, but we'll go ahead and teach you how to work them in the Tri Power program. Identifying weak areas and correcting them early in your training program will allow your major groups like the pecs and lats to contract efficiently.

THE NEUTRAL SPINE

Neutral spine posture is key for proper spinal alignment. Maintaining a neutral spine will decrease the risk of getting an injury and improve your walking efficiency. If you allow yourself to slip out of a neutral spine for any length of time, it will lead to muscular imbalances and limit your performance. Think of your spine like the crankshaft of your car. If the crankshaft is true (and you have proper lubrication), the bearings will last the life of the car. However, if the crankshaft is just slightly off, the bearings will burn out after a few hundred miles.

Finding your neutral spine can be challenging. After all, your spine is not precisely straight. It actually has three natural curves: cervical or neck, thoracic or trunk/torso, and lumbar (lower back). There are two common mistakes in posture: too much anterior tilt (forward) and too much posterior tilt (reverse/flat back).

Begin by lying down on your back on the floor. Bend your knees, feet hip-distance apart and flat on the floor. In this position, the lower back (lumbar) will not be flat against the floor. This is the natural curve of the lower spine. Now, place the heels of your hands on the two bones at the front and top of your pelvis. Make a triangle with your index fingers and thumbs and place them directly over the navel. The hands should be in a horizontal plane. Visualize a glass of water balanced between the triangle. It should remain unspilled in a neutral alignment. If you use your abdominal muscles to press your lower back into the floor, you will experience a posterior tilt. If you overarch your lower back, you will experience an anterior tilt and the water would have spilled out between your legs. Try moving between neutral, posterior, and anterior positions several times. Once you have developed an awareness of the pelvis tilting in this position, attempt it on your hands and knees. The Cat Stretch is a great exercise for this practice.

Get ready to take this awareness into a standing position, and then adapt proper alignment in your swim, bike, and run. First, take a look at your neutral spine in a mirror. We'd like to introduce you to two very important imbalances: the upper and lower cross syndromes.

Upper Cross Syndrome

Generally, upper cross syndrome means a forward slouch in the upper body. We call this a kyphotic or rounded upper torso. This muscle imbalance indicates shortened front muscles in the chest and weak/overstretched muscles in the back and shoulder girdle. The upper cross syndrome can also cause shallow breathing, shortening of the diaphragm, and pinching of the rotator cuff in the shoulder joint.

Lower Cross Syndrome

This syndrome affects 500-miles/week cyclists and office workers alike. It affects your front hip muscles and lower back attachments. Everyone knows at least one person who has that excessive sway back and protruding stomach who walks on the front of their toes.

CORRECTIVE STRENGTH EXERCISES

Tri Power's corrective strength exercises are designed to specifically strengthen muscle groups that have a propensity to fatigue prematurely during triathlons. Our primary areas of concern involve the shoulder girdle, neck/upper arm, back muscles, and outside/inside hip muscles. The exercises in this section will be new to you, so take your time going through and make sure to do everything in perfect form.

An example of the benefits of corrective strength exercises is the shoulder. It's an extremely mobile joint that still requires stability from the rotator cuff. When your arm bone slides around in its socket, the stress on the rotator cuff muscles can be too much. To correct these stressors, you will strengthen the rotator cuff muscles.

Have fun with this section, be patient, and listen to your body during the movements.

Upper Cross Syndrome

CHEST/SHOULDER PNF MOVEMENT, OR DRAWING THE SWORD

Pretend to draw a sword out of your opposite hip, keeping your elbow straight as it crosses the midline of body. Rotate the shoulder and hand from inside/outside fashion with your hand rotated in. An important technique is to keep the shoulder down while the arm is moving through the pattern.

SWIMMING

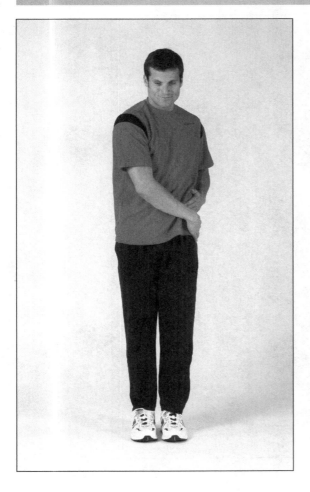
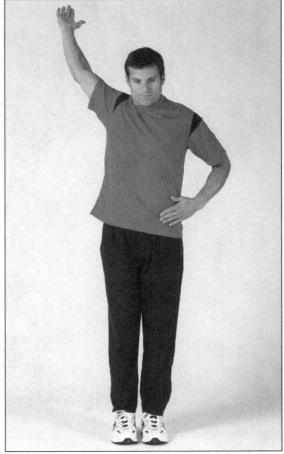

Shoulder Impingement

DUMBBELL PENDULUM ROTATION

Only perform this exercise if you have no history of rotator cuff tears. A primary concern in triathlon is overuse in the shoulder joint, hence pendulum swings will 'open' up the space between the rotator cuff and its bony covering. Find a 5-pound dumbbell. Place it between the middle and index fingers. Bend over, supporting the body with the hand and slowly start to rotate small to big circles with the dumbell counterclockwise.

SWIMMING

Neck Strength

MANUAL RESISTANCE

Sit comfortably, relaxing the hips and legs. Looking straight ahead and keeping the neck aligned with the shoulders, use the hand on the same side as the neck muscle being worked. Gently apply pressure as the head returns to the starting position, not when you are moving your head towards your shoulder.

Variation: Physioball Head Lifts Prone on Ball

SWIMMING

Restricted Neck Extensors

NECK FLEXION WITH ASSISTANCE

In a sitting position, relaxing the hips and legs, place your hands on the front of your thighs. Gently breathe in and drop your chin forward. Feel a stretch through the upper back and the neck. To intensify the stretch, try assisting with the hand behind the head, or slowly round the upper/middle back to incorporate the spine.

BIKING

Strength Neck Flexors
SUPINE NECK LIFTS

Lie on your back and support your head with one arm. Gently lift your forehead vertically, feeling the muscles in the front of your neck contract. The nonsupporting hand can place the fingertips on the forehead to provide biofeedback or resistance.

BIKING

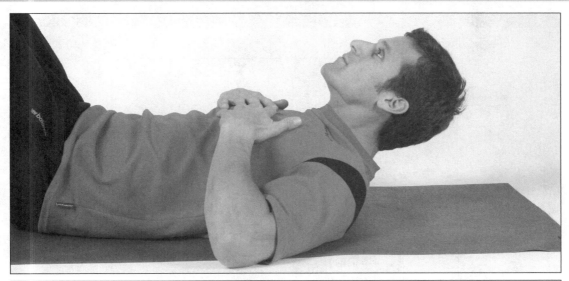

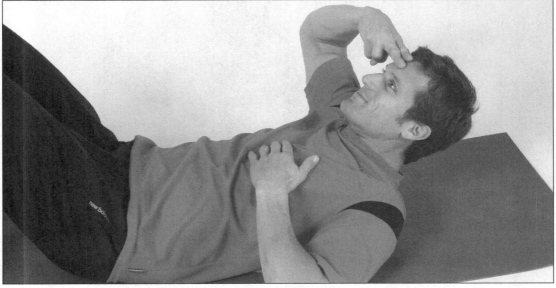

Weak Upper Back Muscles

DOUBLE ARM ELBOW PUSH

The triathlete can execute this movement standing, or kneeling in front of a wall facing outward if preferable. The upper body should be positioned approximately 6 inches from the wall. Take both elbows and push gently into the wall, feeling the upper back contract. Relax the neck and breathe.

BIKING

Weak Upper Back Muscles
SINGLE ARM PRONE ARM LIFT

Lie down on your stomach with one arm along the side of the body and the second arm resting on the ground above the head. Initiate the movement with the second arm by lifting off the ground, palm facing inward. Feel the upper shoulder and middle back contract.

BIKING

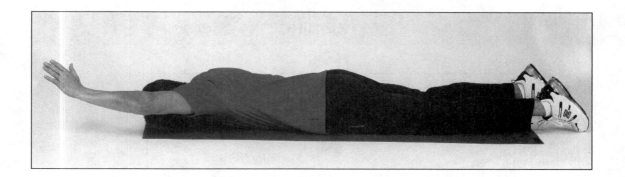

Stability in Rotator Cuff/ Shoulder Joint

DUMBBELL OSCILLATIONS

Lay on your back. With a 3 to 5-pound dumbbell in your working hand, straighten the arm vertically. Draw the arm bone back into the socket by pulling it backward. Once the joint is stable, slowly move the dumbbell around in an alphabet pattern. These small movements enhance the strength of the rotator cuff.

RUNNING

Upper Cross Syndrome

INTERNAL AND EXTERNAL ROTATIONS

Position the working arm with a 90-degree elbow angle. Place a towel (2–3 inches thick) between the elbow and side of the body. For the external movement, begin from the back of the shoulder. For the internal movement, initiate the movement from the front of the shoulder.

ALL SPORTS

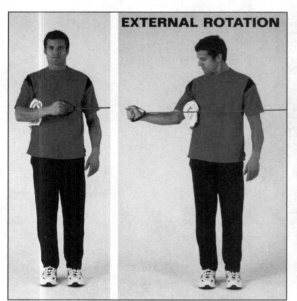

EXTERNAL ROTATION

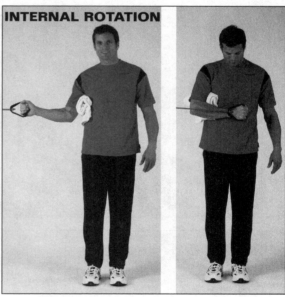

INTERNAL ROTATION

Lower Cross Syndrome and Abdominal Strength

REVERSE CRUNCH

In supine position, place your hands with palms up next to your thighs. Bring knees to your chest and press your lower back to the floor. Lower feet until toes touch the floor and return to starting position. Don't lower your feet further if your lower back comes off the floor.

Variation: Medicine Ball between Thighs

ALL SPORTS

Weak Glutes/Tight Hip Flexor

SUPINE HIP EXTENSION

In a prone position on floor with knees bent, hold your arms by your side with palms facing up. First engage and draw in the abs, then clench the glutes tightly. Slowly lift the hips off floor until the shoulders, hips, and knees are in a direct line. Lower the hips to starting position and begin process again.

ALL SPORTS

As an alternative, try this in a supine position. Extend one leg so that both thighs are parallel and hold for 10 seconds. Another variation in the prone position is to hold a medicine ball or towel between your thighs when lifting them in the air. This second variation is excellent for strengthening the vastus medialis and will help keep proper tracking of the kneecap.

VARIATION 1

VARIATION 2

Hip Stabilizers: Weak Glute Medius

SIDE PLANK WITH BENT BOTTOM KNEE

Lie on your side with your elbow on floor directly under shoulder and legs stacked. Bend bottom knee to 90 degrees. Lift hip off floor and extend top leg so that leg is parallel to floor. Hold position for 30 seconds. Execute twice on each side. Keeping your pelvis stable in this way helps avoid lower back issues and helps performance by avoiding unwanted hip sway.

ALL SPORTS

Tight Hip Flexors
RUNNER'S LUNGE

Place one knee on towel or rolled rubber mat on floor. Extend other leg forward so that it is bent 90 degrees. Extend arm of kneeling side over head. Squeeze the glute of the same leg and gently press hips forward. Do not arch back.

As a variation, try performing these lunges dynamically. Make sure not to bounce trailing knee on floor.

ALL SPORTS

Weak Lower Back

BACK EXTENSIONS

Lie prone, arms by side with back of hands on floor. Rotate toes toward each other to keep the glutes slacked. Lift chest off floor and rotate hands so that the palms face floor. Squeeze shoulder blades back keeping the head aligned with your spine. Rotating the hands and squeezing the shoulders back will engage the throraco-lumbar fascia and help maintain good posture.

ALL SPORTS

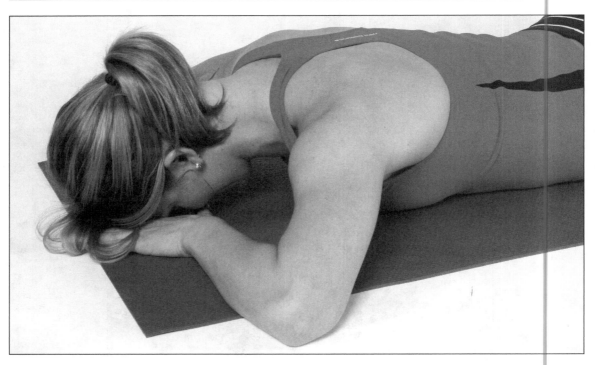

Weak Lower Back

BACK EXTENSION FOR MULTIFIDUS

The multifidus muscle is a deep back muscle that connects vertebrae as they move up the spine. It works in conjunction with the transverse abdominus (TVA) to brace the core and stabilize the back. Lie prone on floor, placing forefinger and thumb together. Place face on hands. Point toes inwardly together. Lift your arms and chest off the floor.

ALL SPORTS

Recovery

9

Recovery is just as much a part of training as the actual event of lifting a weight. It can mean a number of things, from recovery of muscle tissue with nutrition after a strenuous workout to an extended stretching session following an Olympic distance triathlon.

How do the pros recover? Lance Armstrong and the US Postal Team had two massage therapists on staff. While we don't expect you to have access to your own massage therapist, the smart triathlete will be properly rejuvenated for the next effort. Below are some benefits you will enjoy if you pay proper attention to your recovery. We hope it will help you understand why recovery is important if you are planning to remain in this sport for any length of time:

- Increased blood flow and circulation
- Decreased muscle inflammation
- Decreased joint pain
- Faster return to training

After a race, how do those legs feel? If you gave it your all, probably very old. Metabolic by-products create an oxidative effect in your mus-

cles. In other words, this extreme kind of exercise produces inflammation that will lead to sorely fatigued muscles even days after a race. Here are several ways to flush out the residual metabolic waste:

Hydration

One thing we all tend to do less than we should is drink hydrating fluids, or liquids that nourish the body such as water, juices, and replacement drinks. There are nonhydrating fluids, or diuretics, as well, such as coffee, soda, and alcohol. We suggest drinking 12 cups a day for women, and 16 for men. Of course, increase this if you are involved in strenuous activity that involves a lot of sweat and sun.

Massage

A therapist will not grind you body into a pulp after a race. Rather, general tissue movement will create a pumping effect in the body that leads to greater circulation to the heart, lungs, and brain. Our recommendation is a massage within 1 to 6 hours after a race, and additionally stretching and icing sore body parts. Massage will allow the stretching and icing to work more effectively. Here are some of the benefits of massage:

- Increased circulation
- Relaxes and softens injured and overused muscles
- Reduces spasms and cramps
- Increases joint flexibility
- Reduces recovery time for strenuous workouts and eliminates followup pain

Movement

Do not sit down after the race. Instead, use several of our movement-preparation exercises to enhance recovery. Rotate your hips, spine, and shoulders through gentle ranges of motion for 5-10 minutes. Stop immediately if you feel any sharp pains.

Nutrition

Most races serve carbs afterward. This is getting better, but unfortunately too many carbohydrates will lead to stomach cramping and pains, which lead to diarrhea and dehydration. The missing element here is protein. Our recommendation is to balance out the recovery and get at least 1:1 protein and carbs. Your protein should come from natural food sources. Martin J. Gibala, Ph.D., suggests "given that protein has been shown to promote muscle recovery after strenuous exercise, it seems prudent for athletes to consume protein with carbohydrates as part of their recovery nutrition strategy." It's in your best interest to consume a bit of both protein and carbohydrates following strenuous exercise. A heavy meal consisting solely of either one could leave you with an upset stomach.

Heat vs. Ice

Icing a sore area for 10-15 minutes after an extremely fatiguing workout is a smart step to take in the recovery process. A quick and efficient method of icing can be accomplished by freezing Styrofoam cups full of water in the freezer. Once the water is frozen, place a towel next to your skin and rub the fatigued area. As the ice diminishes, just peel back the cup to reveal more ice. It's a great trick to use on the road and is a cost effective and less messy alternative to making or buying ice packs.

Self Myofascial Release (SMR)

This should be performed the day following a race. You will be in a state of inflammation, swelling, and general fatigue. These factors lead to the muscles and joints becoming sore to the touch. The last thing you want to do is apply an aggressive recovery modality such as SMR. Instead, apply the above recovery methods, and once 24 hours or so has passed, gently apply myofascial exercises to your muscles. This will take out the knots that have begun to form in your muscles.

Conclusion

When you reach your goal, whether it's finishing your first triathlon, conquering a new distance, or finishing a phase workout, take pride in the success of the moment. Accomplishment is built on consistency, patience, and faith in that what you are doing is not only good for your body, but for your mind. Are you dedicated enough to start down the path to becoming a triathlete? Can you commit several hours per week to training using the *Tri Power* strength program, along with the guidance of a quality triathlon coach? Get ready, and good luck!

—Paul and Will

Paul Frediani, ACE, ACSM, is a USA Triathlon Level I Certified Coach and author of many fitness books, including *PowerSculpt for Women, PowerSculpt for Men, PowerBand, Golf Flex,* and others. Paul has finished more than 20 triathlons, placing 2nd,3rd, and 5th in Masters Clydesdale division. He has been featured on national television and magazines, including *Fitness, InStyle,* and *Self,* and currently resides in New York City.

William Smith, MS, NSCA, CSCS, MEPD, began coaching triathletes in 1993 and has a career in rehabilitation, working hands-on with athletes and post-rehab clientele. He was a Division I Collegiate Strength Coach and has been competing in triathlons and marathons since 1998, recently finishing the Steelhead Half Ironman in Michigan witha 5 hour 22 minute time. Will currently consults for fitness, healthcare, and wellness centers in New York and New Jersey via Will Power and Fitness Associates, a full-service fitness and educational consulting business.

Appendix A: FAQ

"What is tempo?"

Tempo is the duration of each repetition of an exercise. It dictates the time your muscles are under weight bearing stimulus. For example, one rep of a pushup done at a 3:1:3 tempo would place the muscle under stimulus for 7 seconds. It would mean lowering the body for three counts, holding it at the bottom for one, and pushing up at a three count.

"Why change the tempo of an exercise?"

Slow tempos of 3:1:2 or longer are best for developing deep postural stabilizing muscles, as in Foundations Phase. In Building Phase, we use tempos of 2:1:2. Medium tempos of 2:1:2 are best for strength gains of primary muscle groups. In the Power, Phase the tempo of 1:0:1 is best for developing explosive power.

"How do I know how much weight or load to use?"

Load is the type of resistance that you are overcoming. Examples of load are bodyweight, dumbbells, barbells, cables, medicine balls, and rubber bands—essentially any resistance that your body must overcome. If you find yourself swinging the weight or unable to hold good posture, maintain technique or tempo, or properly stabilize yourself, lighten the load or reduce level of exercise.

What is 'challenging on last rep'?

Challenging on the last rep is not only a description of the difficultly of the movement, but a way to gauge strength progress. To see strength results, you must put your body under stress (load). The last 1-2 reps must be at a level, which is challenging but doable in good form. Your body over time will adapt to the stress of the load. Therefore, you must increase the intensity of the program by manipulating volume, rest, or tempo relative to the phase.

"How many sets are enough?"

This depends on which level of the training cycle you are in—adaptation, strength, power, or maintenance—and what is the specific goal. For adaptation, 1-3 sets. To develop strength, 2-3 sets of heavier weights. For power, 3 sets. 1-3 plus sets of high reps depending on interval time during maintenance.

"How long will it take me to get stronger?"

You may feel stronger within a few weeks, but this is primarily a neural adaptation. Real strength gains take 6-10 weeks.

"Could I be creative with the exercise program?"

Sure, but remember that when you change one of the variables (sets, reps, load, or rest interval), it often means decreasing one or more of the other variables.

"I really enjoy my program— why do I need to change it?"

Well, let's say you have settled into the strength portion of your program, and you don't want to move on to the power section. Your body will adapt to the program over time and you will stop seeing results. We know change is hard, but only by requiring your body to adapt to change will it get stronger.

"Will my muscles get stiff and sore from strength training?"

If you've had little experience with strength training, you may have some initial soreness. Delayed onset muscle sores (DOMS) is a common by-product. Soreness on the following day is from muscle breakdown and inflammation. If sore 48 hours after, it is muscle damage (rebuilds to stronger muscle), which comes from a heavier workout.

"Won't I get bulky from strength training?"

No. Men do have a propensity to put size on but that can be manipulated based on the type of stimulus, a.k.a. heavy or lighter loads.

"I'm short on time. I need to do my strength training either before or after my regular training. Which is best?"

If you strength train before a swim/bike or run you will be prefatigued. You might not get your fastest times. Your technique will suffer but you will be getting stronger by adapting to fatigue. If you do a strength workout directly after a training session your strength workout will most likely not be as high in intensity. Never strength train before a skill workout.

AEROBARS: Bars attached to the front of the handlebars that allow the triathlete to lean forward into a compact aerodynamic position during the cycling component of triathlon.

AEROBIC EXERCISE: Aerobic exercise includes any type of exercise, typically those performed at moderate levels of intensity for extended periods of time. Oxygen is used as the primary energy source.

AGE GROUPER: triathlon s are divided into age divisions. Depending on the size of the triathlon and number of participants, a wide range of age divisions can exist for any given race. Examples of age groups by age are 20–24 or 70 and up.

ANAEROBIC EXERCISE: Anaerobic exercise refers to the initial phase of exercise or any short burst of intense exertion in which the glycogen or sugar is consumed without oxygen, a far less efficient process than aerobic exercise.

ATHENA CLASSIFICATION: A female triathlete who weighs more than 145 lbs. Weight groups are divided into two age groups: an open category for those 39 and under and a masters division for those 40 and over.

CERVICAL SPINE: The seven vertebrae that attach immediately below the head. Head, neck, and shoulders connect to this area.

CLYDESDALE CLASSIFICATION: A male triathlete who weighs more than usually 200 lbs. Weight groups are divided into two age groups: an open category for those 39 and under and a masters division for those 40 and over.

CORE: The core refers to the body minus the legs and arms. Functional movements are highly dependent on the core, and lack of core development can result in a tendency to injury. The major muscles of the core reside in the the belly and the mid and lower back and, moving outward, include the pelvis and shoulder girdle.

FASCIA: Located between the skin and underlying structure of muscle and bone, it is a seamless web of connective tissue that covers and connects the muscles, organs, and skeletal structures in our body. Muscle and fascia are united forming the Myofascial system.

FOAM ROLLER: A therapeutic device used in rehabilitation and fitness conditioning. The roller is a long cylindrical dense foam item used in corrective, core, and strengthening exercise programs.

HALF-IRON MAN DISTANCE: 1.2 mile Swim/56 mile Bike/13.1 mile Run

HIP EXTENSORS: A muscle group located in the back portion of the leg. The hip extensors pull the leg and foot backward in running and help stabilize the pelvis movements with the upper body. Muscles in this grouping are the hamstrings, glutes, and adductors.

HIP FLEXORS: A muscle group that passes through the pelvis that flexes the femur onto the lower back and pelvis. The hip flexors include muscle groups such as the tensor fasciae latae, sartorius muscle, and iliopsoas. The muscles also contribute to flexing the lower back onto the pelvis when the pelvis is fixed or flexing the pelvis onto the lower back when the lower back is fixed.

IRON MAN DISTANCE: 2.4 mile Swim/112 Bike/26.1 Run

IT-BAND SYNDROME: Band of thick connective tissue moving down from the outside of the same side hip to the shin. Rubbing between this tissue and bone can cause extreme pain in the outside of the knee.

ITU LONG COURSE: 3 km Swim/80 km Bike/20 km Run

LOWER CROSS SYNDROME: An imbalance of tight versus weak muscles in the lower portion of the body, specifically the hips.

LUMBAR SPINE: The five vertebrae that attach to the bottom of the vertebral column and sit on top of the pelvis. The lumbar vertebrae are the thickest and most compact, making them very stable. Lower back resonates from this after following long rides and runs.

MYOFASCIAL THERAPY (SELF-MASSAGE/FOAM ROLLING): Myofascial release refers to the manual massage technique for stretching the fascia and releasing bonds between fascia and stuctures such as the muscles and bones, with the goal of eliminating pain, increasing range of motion, and balancing the body. The fascia is manipulated, allowing the connective tissue fibers to reorganize themselves into a more flexible, functional fashion.

OLYMPIC DISTANCE: 1.5 km Swim/40 km Bike/10 km Run

PRIME MOVER MUSCLES: The larger and broader muscles, such as the pectoralis major, are responsible for generating movement, as in a bench press. They create the normal range of movement in a joint by contracting the prime move around the joint. Other examples are the lats, quads, and glutes.

ROTATOR CUFF: A group of four muscles that wrap around the upper portion of the arm bone. Otherwise known by the S.I.T.S. acronym (suprasinatus, infraspinatus, teres minor, and subscapularis), the rotator cuff blends into one common tendon that inserts into the outside of the upper arm.

SPRINT DISTANCE: .5 mile Swim/12.5 mile Bike/3.1 mile Run

STABILIZER MUSCLES: Muscles that provide support across joints, as in the multifidus across spinal vertebrae. Stabilizers tend to be smaller muscles than their primer mover conterparts.

THORACIC SPINE: The twelve vertebrae that attach immediately below the cervical vertebrae. This area is one of the primary 'rotational' of our body, often seen as a 'hump' in poor posture.

TRANSITION AREA: Strategic areas called T1 and T2, as in transition 1 and 2. Between the swim/bike and bike/run, the triathlete will change into biking or running gear as they finish, then prepare for the next element.

UPPER CROSS SYNDROME: An imbalance of tight versus weak muscle groups in the upper portion, specifically the shoulder girdle.

VO2 MAX: VO2 max is the maximum amount of oxygen, in milliliters, one can use in one minute per kilogram of bodyweight. (The derivation is V? - volume per time, O2 - oxygen, max - maximum). It is also called maximal oxygen consumption or maximal oxygen uptake. Expressed either as an absolute rate in litres of oxygen per minute (l/min) or as a relative rate in milliliters of oxygen per kilogram of bodyweight per minute (ml/kg/min), the latter expression is often used to compare the performance of endurance sports athletes.

Appendix C: Triathlon Education and Equipment Resources

SWIMMING RESOURCES AND EDUCATION

Preparing for the swim effectively is one of the pitfalls that tend to affect triathletes, particularly those with no formalized swim training. What we hear quite often is, "Once I get past the swim, I'm fine." The problem with this train of thought is that it negates the inherent importance of the swim from a performance—and more importantly from a safety—standpoint. Not preparing properly for the swim leg, your first event, can leave the triathlete in two precarious positions. First, you will be fatigued, uptight, and nervous before the race. Also, you will be exhausted and spent afterward. This is not a good place to be mentally or physically before hopping on your bike, the second leg. Yet, since this is the shortest of events, many triathletes don't put the time and energy into learning the proper skills it takes to swim effectively. Triathletes new to the sport with a limited background in swimming should be spending an equal amount of time in the pool learning stroke technique and drills. Time on a bike that might shave a few minutes off your total time would be better spent hiring a swim coach or joining a Masters swim team. Swimming harder and longer will simply not make you swim faster with less effort. Leaning proper swim technique will shave minutes off your time. Not only that, but once you "get it", you will look forward

to getting into the water. No more sleepless nights before the race.

There are several pieces of equipment you need for your swim. Let's start with the obvious—a swimsuit. For the purpose of time, it's best to wear a Lycra tri-suit or tri shorts. Lycra is a durable and breathable material that in the form of a tri-suit or shorts can be kept on for the entire race. The suits have a slight bit of padding on the seat for biking. Goggles are not mandatory but we highly suggest them. There are several brands to choose from. They range from $20 to $30. Be sure you purchase and use them beforehand. Don't buy a pair the day before a race unless you know the brand and how they fit. Ear plugs and nose plugs are fine if you're training in a pool and have sensitivity to chlorine. You probably won't need them in an open-water swim unless you're prone to ear infections. A swimming cap most likely will be given to you in your goodie bag in the pre-race check-in area. Often the color of your cap will correspond to the heat, which is generally assigned by age. If you suffer from the cold or the water temperature is below 70 degrees, you may want to use two caps. Or purchase a Hot Head Cap designed for cold water swimming at www.barracudausa.com.

Wetsuits are used more often now than in the past because of performance and the buoyancy one can give an inexperienced swimmer. Wetsuits are not allowed if the water temperature is 78 degrees or above. They come in a variety of designs, including a full-body suit covering the arms and legs, a sleeveless suit with the arms exposed, and a suit with the lower legs and arms exposed. Keep in mind a wetsuit can be challenging to get on and off. It's a good idea to practice getting in and out of the wetsuit. It also helps to buy a product know as Body Glide. It looks like a deodorant stick. You rub it on your legs and arms and it acts as a lubricant, helping the wetsuit to slide off your body easily. Today's modern wetsuits are designed to have great flexibility even throughout the shoulder girdle. Benefits of the wetsuit include buoyancy—they keep your hips high in the water, giving you less resistance and faster times. They are also beneficial to wear if you know that there are jellyfish in the water—a wetsuit protects you from their stings. Of course, wetsuits also keep your body temperature warm. Over all, a wetsuit is quite beneficial to the triathlete and should be included in your repertoire. Visit the resources listed below and educate yourself on the makeup of a wetsuit, then take this information to your local triathlon outfitter for a fitting.

Organizations
United States Masters Swimming
www.usms.org
USMS National Office
P.O. Box 185
Londonderry, NH 03053-0185
Tel: 800-550-SWIM
Fax: 603-537-0204

USA Swimming
www.usaswimming.org
1 Olympic Plaza
Colorado Springs, CO 80909
Tel: 719-866-4578
Fax: 719-866-4669

Web-based Resources
Tri Swim Coach (www.triswimcoach.com)
Swimmersguide.com
Speedo (www.speedousa.com)
Get Fit Now (www.getfitnow.com)

CYCLING RESOURCES AND EDUCATION
Undoubtedly the bike is the most expensive and complex piece of equipment you will invest in. Take heart—with today's modern technology you can find excellent entry-level bikes at about $1,200 that will last you many years.

The most often asked question is, "Do I need a tri bike?" Simply said, "no." You can ride any bike in a triathlon—from a mountain bike to a commuter bike to a hybrid. The question is how fast and how comfortable do you want to be? If you're planning to participate in sprints or Olympic distance triathlons, a road bike with standard 10 speeds and drop bars is a good choice.

A triathlon bicycle is designed for comfort and aerodynamics. The most obvious feature is the handlebars, also known as aero-bars. The aero-bars allow the triathlete to position his or her elbows on rubber cups on the bars. This places the elbows closer together and lowers the torso, placing the triathlete in an aerodynamically appropriate position. The seat post tube is also positioned to engage more of the muscles in the back of your legs, the hamstrings. This lessens the fatigue in the front muscles of the legs—quadriceps—and keeps your legs fresh for your run. Does it sound like a tri bike is for you? Well, not so fast. Although tri bikes are designed for comfort, they are not for everyone. If you lack flexibility in your lower back and trunk, a tri bike will be very uncomfortable and can create lower back strain. You may also find that positioning the hips forward, which lessens the fatigue in the quadriceps and engages more of your hamstrings, may create knee strain. So the first rule of thumb is your comfort. Find a certified USAT or USAC coach and listen to his or her recommendations. But keep in mind that you are the expert when it comes to your comfort on your bike.

Once you decide on your bike, be sure you have an appropriate bike helmet. You won't be allowed to participate in a triathlon

if you do not wear a helmet certified by ANSI, CPSC, or SNELL. A certifying sticker should be on the inside of your helmet. Most helmets purchased in the US within the last two to three years are certified. And just as a reminder, you will be disqualified if your helmet is not properly placed on your head, with the chin strap latched, before removing your bike from the bike rack.

As for bike shoes, we recommend them for two reasons: comfort and economy in your pedal stroke. Bike shoes have hard soles so you don't lose power from your feet to the pedal as you would if you were wearing running shoes. If you do wear running shoes you will need to have cages on the pedals. This isn't so bad if you are doing a sprint distance triathlon—it will make the transition faster from the bike to the run—but what you gain in the transition you will have probably lost on bike.

One last recommendation: Place a ringer or bell on your handlebar, just to remind yourself that triathlons are supposed to be FUN!

Organizations

United States Cycling Federation
www.usacycling.org
USA Cycling Inc.
1 Olympic Plaza
Colorado Springs, CO 80909
Tel: 719-866-4581
Fax: 719-866-4628

Bike Reviews

www.trisports.com/bikes.html
www.trifuel.com
www.all3sports.com
www.trizilla.com
www.gurubikes.com
www.trekbikes.com
www.feltracing.com
www.rooworld.com
www.roadbikereview.com

RUNNING

To most people, running would seem to be the 'easiest' of the three triathlon events. In the swim, we have to worry about getting kicked or swam over, on the bike, we worry about drafting violations, flat tires, and getting safely on and off our bike in the transition area. Although running does not have the inherent 'turmoil' that could occur in the prior two events, it does have its own considerations and preparations that need to be accommodated for in your training program—namely, appropriate footwear, accessories/transition items, and nutrition.

Footwear is the most important component, absent of proper training, in your running program. There are a variety of running shoe manufacturers on the market, including Nike, Mizuno, New Balance, and Asics. Consulting with your podiatrist, pedorthist (shoe-fitting specialist), or a specialty running store will allow you to determine the type of shoe you need. Determining a running shoe will be based on your foot structure, gait pattern or biomechanics during stride, event distance or terrain in some cases, and special considerations such as a pre-existing injury.

An important point to make about running within the triathlon context is it's placement of order amongst the three sports. Following a swim and bike, along with the adrenaline rush that comes with racing, the triathlete can experience mental and physical fatigue unfamiliar to the newbie. This makes it even more important that the running shoe is easy to get on and off and is stable and supportive, while being light enough to pull forward with fatigued lower body muscles. These seemingly modest tips will add up over the course of the run.

Lastly, work on your running form. Running form drills can be done before or after your workout. Two areas that can improve dramatically are your arm swing and leg turnover, both important for speed and running economy. One resource for learning more about simple running drills is United States Track and Field.

Our second important category addresses accessory items. A thorough list of running equipment can be found in our 'Checklist' section located after the Appendices. Accessories consist of headwear, fuel belt, sunglasses, watch, and 'quick locks' for your shoelaces. This is in no way an exhaustive list, rather suggestions for basic equipment. Our suggestions are commensurate upon the distance and climatic considerations. For example, headwear might not be needed when racing in April, or a fuel belt might not be needed when competing in a sprint distance race. These are things that you will learn with practice and racing.

The third category is nutrition. We will all be guilty at one time or another of not eating or drinking enough going into the run. Practicing hydration and eating during training will leave you feeling refreshed after a workout, while recovering faster for the next workout. Use the Gatorade Sports Science Institute as an online resource for nutrition.

Organizations
Road Runners Club of America
www.rrca.org
8965 Guilford Rd, Suite 150
Columbia, MD 21046

New York Road Runners Club
www.nyrr.org
9 East 89th Street
New York, NY 10128
Tel: 212.860.4455

United States Track and Field
www.usatf.org
One RCA Dome, Suite 140
Indianapolis, IN 46225
Tel: 317-261-0500
Fax: 317-261-0481

Appendix D: Triathlon Resources

WEBSITES

www.markallenonline.com
www.willno.com
www.paulfrediani.com
www.getfitnow.com

Expo

Triathlons will generally have an exposition prior to the race. During this expo, which also happens at events such as marathons, the triathlete will pick up his or her race number, important race day information, and a timing chip if applicable. The larger triathlons (by size, not necessarily by distance) usually do not offer race day packet pickup because this would create a state of 'hysteria' on race day. If you are coming in from out of state and cannot arrive until after the expo closes on the day before the race, call ahead to the race director or find out if your registration information can be sent via mail. Two other important points here: First, you will need to be 'marked'. It is a branding by race coordinators done with a marker. Look for them to write your age on an arm and calf muscle. This branding will stay with you for several days and prove to all of your doubters a triathlete is in their midst. Secondly, the expo is a great place to pick up nutritional products, consult with a bike mechanic, and purchase discounted clothing. DO NOT use any new nutritional products the day before or during the race—this could ruin your entire experience if the food/drink doesn't agree with your stomach.

Transition Areas

The transition area is where triathletes will report on race morning. This staging area allows the triathlete to arrange the bike and running gear in a predetermined rack position. Once you determine your race number (given at the expo), find the assigned rack spot for your bike. Try to identify your bike with something, a bright colorful object for instance, that will bring the bike into your sights quickly when you come out of the water into Transition I after the swim.

Play around at home with practice setups. Imagine the confusion of hundreds of triathletes running around after the swim, looking for their bike and running attire. You MUST be organized and prepared, as this will ease nerves and anxiety. As Sun Tsu says, "The battle is won before it is ever fought." Well, you still have to race, but take comfort knowing you have practiced your transition at home numerous times, have alternative plans if something goes awry, and have trained hard preceding the race. This knowledge gives you confidence to fall back on.

Tri Power readers will find a pre-race and race day checklist. Use this as a template to plan the items you will need. Absent of your regular nutritional products such as gels and electrolytes, which can be purchased at the expo, try to pack all necessary gear at home before leaving for your race. Copy this list and keep it around for reference.

Race Day Checklist

SWIM STUFF

- ❑ Swimsuit
- ❑ Wetsuit and Pam (for anti-chafing)
- ❑ Wetsuit bag
- ❑ Goggles (defog)
- ❑ Swim cap (usually provided)
- ❑ Sunscreen
- ❑ Towel to wipe sandy feet
- ❑ Cash

BIKE STUFF

- ❑ Pain medicine, earplugs, sunscreen
- ❑ Bike
- ❑ Vitamins, minerals, amino acids, etc.
- ❑ Helmet
- ❑ Cycling shorts

MAIN BIG BAG

- ❑ Bike shoes
- ❑ Toilet bag(soap,toothbrush,razor,etc)
- ❑ Jersey or singlet
- ❑ Alarm clock
- ❑ Cycle gloves
- ❑ Warm clothes, jacket
- ❑ Vaseline or other anti-chafe substance
- ❑ Workout clothes, shorts, T-shirts
- ❑ Sunglasses
- ❑ Shoes, sandals
- ❑ Pump and patch kit
- ❑ Sewing kit, tape, scissors, marker
- ❑ Water bottles
- ❑ Race day food
- ❑ Tools
- ❑ Towels
- ❑ Lock
- ❑ Tools
- ❑ Wash pan and towel
- ❑ Heart rate monitor
- ❑ Floor pump

RUN

- ❑ Shoes
- ❑ Socks
- ❑ Shorts
- ❑ Singlet and race number (pins)
- ❑ Cap
- ❑ Sunglasses (second clean pair)

Appendix E: Sources

Bompa, Tudor, Carrera, Michael. *Periodization Training for Sports, 2nd Edition.* Human Kinetics Publishers: 2005.

Boyle, Mike. *Mike Boyle Strength and Conditioning: Torso Training Manual.* Winchester, MA: May 2000.

Chek, Paul. *Scientific Core Conditioning Correspondence Course Kit.* C.H.E.K. Institute: 1998.

Clark, Andrew. *Dynamic Warm-ups.* IDEA: 2006.

Colgan, Michael. *Real Abdominal Power: Train from the Inside Out.* www.musculardevelopment.com: 2000.

Marek, S.N., et al. 2005. Acute effects of static and proprioceptive neuromuscular facilitation stretching on muscle strength and power output. *Journal of Athletic Training,* 40 (2) 94–103.

Norris, M. Christopher: *Abdominal Training, Second Edition: A Progressive Guide to Greater Strength.* The Lyons Press: 2002.